THE WHEELMAN'S DAUGHTER

Also by Pamela Bauer Mueller

The Kiska Trilogy

The Bumpedy Road
Rain City Cats
Eight Paws to Georgia

Historical Novels

Neptune's Honor
An Angry Drum Echoed
Splendid Isolation
Water To My Soul
Lady Unveiled
A Shadow of Hope
Fly, Fly Away
The Sky Is My Home

The Wheelman's Daughter

Pamela Bauer Mueller

Piñata Publishing

Copyright © 2025 Pamela Bauer Mueller

All right reserved. No part of this book may be used or reproduced in any manner whatsoever without prior written permission except in the case of brief quotations embodied in reviews.

Piñata Publishing
626 Old Plantation Road
Jekyll Island, GA 31527
(912) 635-9402
www.pinatapub.com

Library of Congress Cataloging-in-Publication Data

Bauer Mueller, Pamela
The Wheelman's Daughter / Pamela Bauer Mueller.
Includes bibliographical references and index.

Library of Congress Control Number: 2024953041

ISBN 978-0-9809163-8-6

Cover art by Gini Steele
Typeset by Vancouver Desktop Publishing Centre

This story is dedicated to my Savior: Jesus Christ. Thank you for the abundant blessings You've given us. We know everything comes from you.

"Do not be anxious about anything, but in everything by prayer and supplication with thanksgiving let your requests be made known to God. And the peace of God, which surpasses all understanding, will guard your hearts and your minds in Christ Jesus."
—Philippians 4:6-7

"My race needs no special defense, for the past history of them in this country proves them the equal of any people anywhere. All they need is an equal chance in the battle of life."
—Robert Smalls, November 1, 1895

"Strength and dignity are her clothing,
And she smiles at the future."
—Proverbs 31:25

AUTHOR'S NOTE

I have always had a passion about reading well-written books. Because of that, I became a writer. This career has been a blessing to me in so many ways, including the company of many creative, caring supporters. Writing is a solitary pursuit, but greatly enriched by love given and received. Thank you for reading my stories.

I like to surprise myself each time I write a new book. At this point in life, I've learned that writing is an act of faith, knowing that the right words will appear when I need them. But as an author, I have the responsibility to safeguard my protagonist's story and make it genuine.

History is a conversation between the present and the past. This story is another southern story, written about a woman very few people have heard of or read about. My mission will be to bring her to life and share her true story.

Because I write about real people and true events, I've found that by utilizing dialogue, I'm able to improve the narrative to enhance the character's development. People ask me where I get my dialogue. I find it in letters my characters have written and received, journals and diaries they've kept, and their points of view. I uncover this in my research. I often convert their "written words" into "spoken words," offering you a better understanding of their feelings and values.

I'm happiest when I'm challenged. As you can imagine, I spend many hours doing research. The research phase is when I learn, and the challenge begins. What will I include? Who is relevant in her life? Did she have role models to encourage her? If the person is well-known, the research process is usually time-consuming, but not too difficult to research. If she is not well-known, as in the case of Lizzie Smalls Bampfield, it becomes very laborious and demanding. Yet the challenge energizes me, and once I understand my character, she gets my full attention and becomes a pleasure to reveal.

The accurate setting of every story is paramount. This is where the protagonists make decisions that often reshape their futures. I strive to keep the story personal, including the events and times they lived in during our country's history.

All the people in this story are real and the historical events are accurate. The strong friendship between Frederick Douglass and Lizzie's father, Robert, is factual. I only "created" one person—her best friend Renata Giudici. I know Lizzie would have had a best friend, but could never find out who she was. To keep the story moving, I created Renata's character and placed her in the story. All the other characters were real people, including some slaves whose last names I never knew.

The book Lizzie and her children wrote is also a figment of my imagination, although she very well could have written it. Maybe one day it will be discovered. Lizzie's bravery, love and resilience deeply touched my heart. Uncovering her story brought me deep personal peace. I hope she becomes an inspiration to each of you.

PROLOGUE

Elizabeth

1872

The night seemed darker than usual so the big moon shone more brightly. As we walked down through moon shadows, Mama gripped my hand tightly and hoisted Robbie a little higher on her hip. I felt sleepy but knew we were in a hurry, so I tried to show Mama I was big enough to walk faster so she wouldn't need to pull me anymore.

"Let's stop next to this tree and catch our breath," whispered Mama. As soon as Robbie was steady on a little flat spot, she reached down and pulled out some bread and cider from the folds of her dress. "Eat this, Lizzie, while I feed Robbie."

I nodded and watched her carefully. "And remember, please whisper." She was speaking softly in our Gullah language.

I nodded and looked around me, noticing we were the only ones on the streets. "Mama, where's Daddy?" I asked.

"Hush, Lizzie. We will meet him on his steamer."

Robbie squirmed and began to cough. Mama scooped him up to muffle the sound. He finally settled down to nurse, reaching out to squeeze and release my fingers.

How can I remember all these details and sensations, this soon after my fourth birthday? This extraordinary night is still very clear in my memory, even years later. My father has told me we've discussed it so much that the details are rooted in my brain. My mind can still smell the fumes and hear the sound of distant whistles blowing across the water.

Fog was covering our boat when we arrived at the dock. I ran up to Daddy and hugged him as he lifted me up into his sinewy arms. "Welcome little one. Are you ready to take a ride?"

Glancing over his shoulder, I saw my Mama's other daughter Clara Jones, all of thirteen-years-old.

"Clara, where's Charlotte and Emily?" I asked. Clara and Charlotte were Mama's first daughters, born before she met my Daddy. Charlotte's daughter Emily wasn't with her.

"They stayed back at the house. Emily is too young to come."

I shook my head. "No she's not. She's older than me and I'm here. Why?"

No one answered me so I sat down and tried to understand their conversation. When that got confusing, I rested my head on Mama's lap and closed my eyes.

I woke up when I heard other women, the wives of some of the crew members, speaking excitedly. Daddy was finally telling them what we were planning to do, and they were arguing about missing curfew. Two of them wanted to get off the boat immediately, before they got into more trouble.

Daddy tried to stay calm, but when a few of them started weeping and moaning, he raised his voice.

"Listen to me. You have to trust me. I have spoken to the men onboard and we agreed that this is an opportunity we must take. There will be no turning back now."

Sensing my growing agitation, Mama sat me on her lap. Daddy talked to us calmly about our freedom, then led us to the ship's stateroom where we were told to wait. The others probably knew more by then, but I didn't. Not yet. I trusted my Daddy and Mama. I reached over to cuddle my sleeping brother so Mama and Daddy could talk.

Bits and pieces of their conversation stayed with me. Quietly, Daddy told the others that his plan was dangerous, but if we had faith, it would all be worth the risk. "If we do nothing for our families tonight, we can be broken up and sold separately…or even worse. This is our only chance to be free."

Those last eight words, spoken softly and solemnly, had an immediate effect on the others.

Someone asked, "And if we get caught?

Daddy took several moments to answer. "We already discussed this."

After a brief pause, he looked at each one of us earnestly.

"If necessary, we will hold hands and jump overboard, drowning together in the sea." When the alarmed gasps and muffled interruptions calmed down, some of them started praying. I watched my elders silently.

The ship crept silently away from the dock, making soft slurping noises as the waves lapped against the wharf. The low country grasses along the water might have been waving farewell. The distant chimes of St. Michaels Church warned that curfew had begun for the slaves in the city. Someone muttered what we were all thinking: "Curfew has started. We are breaking the law."

A welcoming breeze moved the warm humid air around us. A faint whistle out on the water told me we had reached another dock. We were quietly led to another ship.

We waited in the small boat *Etowah* while Daddy worked on *The Planter*. Mama told me that Daddy would pilot it and take us to the Union lines.

Three crew members accompanied us across a gangplank. Then we all hid below, until *The Planter* was ready and some of Daddy's crew could return to pick us up. The ship's hold smelled like pluff mud at low tide, so I breathed in the mixed odors of fish, oysters and decay.

Mama settled me and the others around her.

"You've heard the story of Moses in the Bible," she began. "His family and the other Hebrew people had to run away from Egypt to become free." I noticed she was watching the older children, but she kept her fingers interwoven with mine while she spoke.

"They were very frightened but they trusted Moses to lead them. He was a great believer in God, and completely trusted Him."

Clara turned to her mother. "How far did they have to run to become free?"

Mama smiled. "They walked for many days, all the way to the Red Sea. They had to get to the other side, but it was too deep and too wide."

"Mama, what did they do?" I asked, although I had heard the story often at bedtime.

"They prayed, like we're doing tonight. And they believed their prayers would be answered, like we're taught in our churches."

One of the other women shook her head in agreement. "And they knew that God had a special love for slaves like themselves. Their faith kept them strong."

Mama nodded, softly releasing her breath. She was relieved that she'd been able to calm them a little. She knew there was much more in store for us that night, so she quietly prayed for courage.

"And then what happened?" Clara asked again.

"When they reached the sea, Moses stretched out his hand and the waters divided down the middle. The Hebrews passed through on dry land. The Egyptians followed them, but God told Moses to hold up his hands once more. The sea waters rushed over the Egyptian soldiers and they all drowned."

"And what about their freedom?" asked another woman.

Mama smiled. "Then they were slaves no longer."

"And that's what the Lord will do for us," added a crewman.

"Amen," smiled Mama. "Amen."

We waited on the *Etowah* while Daddy finished preparations on *The Planter*. When he finished his work, he steered it toward us very quietly to avoid suspicion. Three men, five women and three children climbed off the *Etowah* and boarded *The Planter*.

We were sent below deck. I quickly fell asleep, but I think Robbie and I were the only ones who were able to sleep. As I drifted off to sleep, I overheard men talking about the need to pass quickly by Ft. Sumter, but I can't remember what else they talked about.

I slept fitfully. At some point I heard a whistle blowing—two long blows and a short one. I looked for Mama and found her on her knees praying, holding the hand of another woman as tears slipped down their cheeks.

Then nodding and smiling, she whispered, "We made it past the fort. The Lord is with us."

The paddle wheels were churning; steam and smoke filled the air as we picked up speed. Sleep found me once more as *The Planter* headed through the dark waters toward the Union ships.

Our unforgettable adventure had just begun.

ONE

Hannah

Sometimes, my life feels like a twisted tangled spool of goat wool. If I pull out the knots from one area, more knots appear somewhere else.

Even my past feels that way. I only know what my mama told me, and that is a complicated story. She came from Africa, but she doesn't know from where. She still has nightmares where she sees herself and a little boy and girl clinging together and crying. "We were hungry all the time," she remembers, wiping a tear from the corner of her eye.

As we sat and polished Missus Kingman's silver, Mama would tell me stories about Anansi, an African spider God. The language she speaks to me is mostly Gullah, but she wants me to help her speak better English, so sometimes we switch back and forth.

"Ole Anasi be tricky an' smartah den de rest of de Gods. He keep his enemies away by his wit and help us slaves wen he kin." She knew I loved these stories.

Mama taught me how to sew and mend clothes, and even as a young child, I helped her work. One afternoon she made a mistake and ripped out a seam to re-do it. At that moment Missus Kingsman walked into the room and rushed over to see what happened.

"Sadie, are you stupid?" she shouted. "That's one of my best gowns, and you've ruined it!" She picked up a switch and lashed it across Mama's face.

My hand flew to my mouth as I screamed and ran to help my mama. I was gasping for breath when Missus Kingsman lunged at me, thrashing me three or four times across my arms as she backed me into the wall.

"Sadie, teach your daughter her place in this world," she shrieked. "And remember yours as well!"

Throwing down the switch, she stormed out. I hurried over to Mama to clean up the blood from her face and body.

"Oh Mama," I sobbed. She hurt you bad." Mama was bent over, whimpering with pain. I felt a hot fury I'd never known before, gasping for breath through my mouth as I tried to stop the bleeding.

One of Mama's eyes was swollen shut for a long time. When she eventually healed, she managed to make a joke of it. "I kin see bettah wif jus' one eye," she told me. She warned me to stay "in my place" around that woman and speak to her as little as possible.

I was a house slave, but several years later I began looking for a way to work outside the house, at least during the day. I was determined to keep my children and my mother safe, housed and fed. Mama still worked for the masters so we were all cared for.

It took me a long time to gather the courage to talk to Master Kingsman about working somewhere else.

It wasn't as difficult as I thought it would be. Instinct pushed me forward. Master Kingsman listened, rubbing his chin while considering my request.

"I'll think it over, since you'll be bringing your salary to me," he answered with his nose in the air.

Through a friend in the church congregation, I managed to find work in a hotel as a room cleaner, doing the hardest assignments and being helpful wherever I could.

Gradually, I made friends with other cleaners, especially a younger woman named Sarah. We worked well enough together to be promoted to laundry, interacting with fewer women so we had time to form a strong bond.

Sarah and I talked about everything. She was nine years younger than I, so young men were on her mind. I had my family to look after, so I just listened politely to her chatter and kept my opinions to myself.

In less than two years, I was in charge of the entire laundry operation in the Planter Hotel in Charleston. Sarah and I often met after work and walked home together.

"Let's get some fruit today," she suggested one afternoon. "I have a little extra money, so I want to use it to buy some oranges and honeydew melon."

That's the day I met Robert, waiting in line across from us at the market. "Well, hello Sarah," he called out.

"Hello yourself, Robert. Are you off work already?"

He chuckled and I noticed his beautiful dark eyes and bushy brows. "No, just getting something to eat before I go back to the docks." Nodding at me, he said, "What's your name?"

I was surprised by his direct question. "My name is Hannah. I'm Sarah's friend." I liked his deep voice. His handsome face, broad shoulders and slim waist were nice to look at too.

Sarah paid for her fruit and took my arm. "Let's go, Hannah. We need to get on home."

"I hope to see you again," he said as we walked away. I glanced over my shoulder and saw him watching us leave. As I turned, he lifted his hand and threw me a grin and a wink.

"Do you know him well?" I asked.

"I've talked to him a few times here and there. Why?"

"He's young, isn't he? But quite handsome."
Sarah laughed. "Yes, he is. Are you interested?"
I shook my head. "No, but he seems smart and cheerful. You don't see that often in young men."
It didn't take long before he saw me again. He must have found out my working schedule. We started walking around Charleston together on Sunday evenings, and sometimes, went to church afterward. We slowly learned a lot about each other. He was only seventeen-years-old and I was thirty-two, with two children from a past relationship a few years back. One day I would explain that part of my life to him, and if he was still interested, I might introduce him to my mother and daughters.

"Hannah, I really like you. I love your sparkling eyes, your shiny black curls, the way you walk, your confidence. And your sassiness! You make me laugh and give me something to look forward to."

He fascinated me with his strong curiosity and thirst for learning new things. His air of self-confidence intrigued me. He wanted to learn to read, but it was prohibited for slaves. He wondered why I wasn't resentful that slaves were not allowed to learn to read.

"I would like to get an education too, Robert, but it's not possible now. Maybe one day."

He told me how he arrived in Charleston, and then explained about his job at the docks. He started as a deck hand and was promoted to piloting a steamer. Because he was a slave, he wasn't called "Captain." Unless you were white or a free slave, your title was "Wheelman." So I gave him the nickname of "Cap."

One evening, sitting together near the water, he said that my quiet wisdom reminded him of his mother, and he wanted me to meet her.

That was a huge surprise. "Oh Cap, it's too soon for that. You sound so serious."

He slipped his fingers through mine. "I am, dear Hannah." His dark eyes shone as he studied my face. "I'm tired of saying goodbye to you every week. We should be married, Sugar. Have our own place together."

Totally shaken by his unexpected declaration, I told him that we needed to slow down. I had to think about our different situations, our families, and whether it was possible to have a future together. He reluctantly agreed, giving me a sweet smile.

But I did agree to meet Robert's mother, Lydia, about whom he spoke fondly. I was curious too.

I liked Lydia immediately. "You carry yourself like African royalty—with dignity and class," she told me. I wondered if she said that because I'm a little taller than Robert, so I asked her.

"No, Hannah," she smiled. "I can see your confidence and strength." I felt the same way about her.

Walking me home, we listened to the mocking bird making a racket in the crepe myrtle bush. Robert stopped abruptly and pulled me close. Whispering, he fixed his gaze on my face. "Sugar, I need a wife. No more running around."

His thumb rested on my chin. "Someone to care for me, and who I can take care of. I need you."

He lowered his head until his face filled my vision. "If we get married, we can work together until I could purchase you and your girls from Master McKee. I overheard him talking about that with some other men."

Trembling with excitement, I managed to keep my voice steady.

"Oh Cap, I can't believe we could ever do that. I've never even dared to dream it."

Robert tipped my chin up, close enough to make me feel safe. I watched as his eyes moved up and down my face. My eyes closed when his lips met mine.

That was our first thrilling moment as a couple—filled with uncertainty, self-denial, desire, and a little fear of all that was to come.

I finally found words to encourage him. "My dear Cap, this might be the right time for us to move forward together," I murmured, feeling much more confident than I could communicate. My feelings were bursting with hope for our new shared future.

TWO

Lydia

My second son came into the world with a bang, screaming all the way. I was forty-three years old. I birthed him in my sparse slave quarters, hidden behind an elegant white frame house sheltered by moss-covered oak trees. After four or five hours, a mid-wife arrived to help me. It had been twenty-one years since I gave birth to his brother Larry. And only three weeks ago, I served as mid-wife to my Missus Jane's first child, Elizabeth Jane. Missus Jane labored for nine hours and finally, I placed a wet and healthy baby in her arms.

But this birth was difficult. Tears rolled down my cheeks as I gasped from the pain and fear for my baby. Fear because as a slave child, I knew he would live a life dictated by someone else. While I tossed and moaned, I remembered hearing the word "tribulation" from the balcony of my church in town. The preacher had said it meant testing our faith and devotion to God. That it is all about the many hardships, trials, and suffering that believers encounter in their lives.

Pushing, screaming, and squeezing my mid-wife's hand, I could feel my flesh loosen and tear. Then I smelled my warm blood spreading onto the sheets under me.

"You git yo'self a big boy, Lydia, and he be right hungry." She soothed my brow as he thrashed his arms and made sucking noises in the air.

I smiled through my tears. "If there be glory in pain, this son of mine... I know he be it."

I named him Robert Henry, as my Missus and Master had requested. They had only one daughter and wanted my child to carry the name of Robert Henry.

My milk came in that evening, and my baby drank and thrived. Something about my boy made me feel like I was chosen.

~

I had been born into slavery at Ashdale Plantation on Lady's Island and grew up in a small wooden cabin with dirt floors and a tabby chimney. As a child I had gathered firewood and plants for cooking, learned to weave sweetwater baskets, helped Mama with her chores, and invented games and toys whenever I could. I also worked in the fields for about four years. My family received a meager amount of clothing: usually two sets of clothes—one for winter and one for the summer.

We got weekly rations of corn and molasses, as well as some meat and rice. Mama told me they allowed us to grow corn and sweet potatoes in little plots for our family. We fished for food and sometimes had pigs and chickens to sell for extra money. We could also trade what we raised, so we ate better than some of the other slaves. I enjoyed taking care of the animals, but I hated seeing them killed for food or being put up for sale. If we sold them, we could keep the money and buy more clothing, tobacco, molasses, and sugar.

Because I was a slave, it was forbidden by law for me to learn how to read. But I loved music, so Mama taught me how to dance. She took me to the little church on the plantation to learn about God, and to sing and dance with the other slaves. Mama told me this church was involved in the Second Grand Awakening. She said our preacher had no schooling but could marry and bury us. For about ten years, I almost never saw a white person, except when Master McKee came by to oversee his crops.

Mama taught me not only our Gullah language, but also the "King's English," because she was a house servant for educated masters and had learned how to speak the language while she worked inside the house. Mama and I spoke Gullah between ourselves and with the other slaves. In the Gullah dialect, we called house servants "Swonga people" and they were considered slave elite. Because Mama saw the white man's world up close, she was a link between the majority of the field slaves and the whites.

"Lydia, you have to learn to talk fine, so nobody thinks you ain't smart."

She educated me in Gullah so I could understand my roots. Gullah is an English-based Creole language created by enslaved West-Africans living in the Sea Islands. Gullah is also a culture—just called "Gullah." This culture came from the customs of men and women who had been kidnapped from their homes in West and Central Africa, beginning in the late 1600s.

The Gullah people belonged to various ethnicities, including the Igbo, Bakongo, Wolof and more. They spoke different languages and practiced different traditions. When they were forced to come together and harvest rice, indigo and cotton, they formed a common language and culture that preserved some aspects of their former lives, including deep spiritual, musical and story-telling traditions. This helped them maintain their identities and connections to each other.

When I was about ten years old, Mama told me that Master John McKee would be taking me to his home in Beaufort to look after his five children. We were both very sad to learn about this separation. Mama reminded me that they had treated both of us well enough, and she was proud that I had been "recruited" among the other young female slaves to work the easier chores of the domestic slave. "We must consider this a blessing, Lydia. God will find a way for us to stay close." It turned out that she was right. After a short time, they permitted me to visit her on certain weekends, and sometimes she came to see me.

A few months before I left, my dear mama reminded me to seek out opportunities to become fluent in the "King's English," so people would take me seriously. She re-told the many stories of Anansi—the spider God of Africa, so I could think of them whenever I missed her. "He be the cleverest creature in da world. Sometime he grow so big as a giant. Oder time he keep so tiny so he kin move from da land to da sky. Now listen to what happen wif de leopards an' de bees." Before finishing the new story, Mama lifted my hand and kissed it. "Baby, we gotta be clever like Anansi. Our world be full of leopards and bees."

When I moved to Beaufort, I wanted to learn everything I could about everything. Missus Margaret McKee would sometimes tell me a little history as we worked together. I felt proud that she wanted me to know about her island of Beaufort.

"Lydia, Beaufort is one of the many Sea Islands off the coast of South Carolina. It sits on a curve of the Beaufort River. It's also the oldest settlement in our state after Charleston. It was chartered in 1711."

She turned and glanced at my face. "Do you understand what I'm telling you?"

I shook my head. "No, Missus. What means chartered?"

MissusMcKee smiled. "It means became a part of South Carolina in 1711."

Then she talked about slavery, and how it had been temporarily stopped in the 1780's because of an economic depression. "But," she continued, "the planters needed the slaves so they smuggled thousands into the country. And, by 1803, the planters succeeded in pressuring the state legislature to re-open the slave trade."

I understood most of this, and wondered how she felt about my people being forced to come here from Africa. For some reason, I didn't ask her that.

She must have read my mind. "Does it make you sad to hear the slaves' history?" she asked gently.

I felt confused and told her so.

"Do you feel comfortable with your life here? I know you miss your mama, but we take you to see her often. Does that make it better?"

I nodded and looked away.

"I wonder if you understand the concept of being 'owned.' You and your mama are our property and belong to us. Along with about one hundred other slaves. We take care of you and meet your needs."

I lifted my eyes to search hers. She looked kind and gentle as she told me these things. I was smart enough to understand that life could be worse for me. The hardest part was living away from Mama, but I was growing up with the children I cared for and we all treated each other well.

Missus McKee stood up and put down her quilting needles. "Now I will check the kitchen in preparation for dinner." She started to go, then turned to look back at me. "I hope we can have some more time to learn together. You are a smart child. I believe you can educate me as well," she said, softly shutting the door behind her.

THREE

Robert

Looking back on my childhood is a bitter-sweet experience. My mother, Lydia, was an important house servant who had helped raise the masters' children. She even assisted in their births as a midwife. We lived with George—the family driver who I called "Uncle," in a two-room cabin behind our master's house.

Master Henry McKee took a liking to me as a little boy, and found numerous and wonderful opportunities to include me in his family's activities. In my youth, he taught me to ride horses, fish, crab, hunt with a gun and swim in the rich estuaries surrounding our island. He included me as his guide and companion. I was able to learn all about local tides and river waters, and I formed a lifelong bond with Missus McKee at the same time. But I also had many tasks to do. Often their children joined me when I pumped water, carried logs, inspected the crops, set up fires, and performed other activities.

I led the McKee children and kept track of them, like an older brother. Their parents allowed me to be a playmate to the two older ones, Elizabeth Jane and William. I grew up in an unusual, but not uncommon, pattern of closeness with this family. My Master became my father figure for the first eleven years of my life. Their daughter, Elizabeth, and I were born just three weeks apart. She and I had similar temperaments and cared about each other like brother and sister.

I was obviously different from them, because I was a slave. They learned to read and write and I could not because of a government restriction on slaves. They did not have a curfew and I did, so when the church bell rang, I had to return to my cabin. Sometimes, I refused to go in when the bell rang. Because of this stubbornness, I was arrested several times, and Master McKee had to go to the jail and get me released. Mama was mortified and decided that something had to be done. She thought I was being raised as a "privileged slave," and that deeply concerned her.

"Son, you know that you are not free. You've been given a good life here with the McKees. The master and missus care for you, almost like a son. But the world won't treat you like they do."

"I know, Mama," I answered, feeling ashamed to have put her in this position. "But at least I'm able to learn things I might have never known just working the fields."

She sat still and silent and gave a mournful shake of her head. "Do you even understand how other slave boys your age live?"

She knew I did not, so she took me to the Beaufort jail yard and made me watch the public beating of slaves. She sat me on her shoulders so I could look over the wall, where I saw a young woman getting a whip lashing, her wrists tied to the lowest branches of a tree. I was horrified and closed my eyes, but I certainly heard her cries from the torture. When the jailor untied her wrists, she fell to the ground, limp and bleeding.

"Oh Mama, why? What have they done to be whipped?" My mother put me down to wipe away my tears.

"Robert, it doesn't matter if they've done nothing. They belong to their masters and if their masters want to teach them a lesson, they can. Or they can sell them or beat them to crush their spirits. That is part of being a slave."

This was the beginning of my personal and dramatic education of what slavery really was. My strong sense of justice rebelled against the horrific reality of bondage.

A few months later, I was taken to the slave auction at the market. This time my Uncle George took me, warning me in advance what I would see.

"Git over here, boy, and git your eyes full." His voice was full of sorrow.

At first, I didn't understand what was happening. He explained. "Slaves are sold to de person who bid de most money. He buys all o jes' part of de family an' kin split dem up. Dey be washed an' oiled up an' stand rite dere, on de platform. Buyers inspect dem and poke dem and open der mouths to see der teeth. De buyers wif de mos' moneys git de slaves dey want."

"And then they are separated from their families?" I asked in disbelief.

"De buyers want only de strongest an' mos' healthy. De families cry an' scream but usually don't git to leave together."

I looked away from him. We watched as one family was bid on. Only three of the seven would be taken. I asked George to take me home.

―――

When I turned eleven, Mama and Master McKee discussed my future. Mama didn't want me to start working in the fields, so she asked him if he could send me to Charleston. He agreed that it was a good idea. Then I could learn other types of work and even make a little money. After he spoke with his wife's married sister, Eliza Ancrum, he asked me to ride with him over his fields.

"Robert, you know that I've allowed you to live with your mother until you are twelve years of age. She's asked me not to send you to work in the fields, because you've not been raised up with the slaves out there. So, I have decided to send you to Charleston. You can stay with my wife's sister, and you can find some type of work up there. Your salary will come back to me, but I'll let you keep a dollar each week. How does that sound to you?"

Turning sideways in the saddle, he checked out my reaction.

"Yes Sir, Mas' Henry. Thank you, Sir. I would like to work on the water."

He laughed in surprise and delight. "Well, I haven't gotten that far yet. Why don't we take a trip over there soon and see what they might be looking for?"

Several weeks later we rode to his plantation on Lady's Island, where Master McKee planned to stay and work for two days. I ate dinner with several slaves who had recently arrived. These young men had learned to read and told me about a man named Frederick Douglass, who was their hero.

"Where did you learn to read?" I asked, not really believing such a life could be possible for a slave boy.

"We lived with a pastor's family whose daughter taught us to read and write after our work was done. They talked about Mr. Douglass, and showed us copies of some of his speeches.

I was excited to see these speeches, but I felt frustrated that I couldn't read them. One of them offered to read parts of it to me.

> *The law gives the Master absolute power over the slave. He may work him, flog him, hire him out, sell him, kill him. In the law, the slave has no wife, no children, no country, no home. He can own nothing, possess nothing, acquire nothing, but what he has must belong to another.*

I fervently absorbed these words. I wanted to know more. I was restless to move to Charleston, where I knew I would find opportunities to learn and grow. Maybe even find a way to learn to read.

The older slave watched me absorbing the words of Douglass. "Robert, I see that your English is excellent, and you have good eating manners. How is that?"

"I am a house slave rather than a field slave. I mostly did indoor work, and domestic labor. My mother made sure I watched and listened to the masters of our home and their children, so it would be easier for me to pick up their habits. It was not difficult to become aware of their white culture." I smiled warmly at them. "My mama says she was able to pass along some European culture to me and take some herself."

Another man sitting on a bench spoke up. "Your mama must love you very much. And your master seems to care about your future as well."

I told them I would be going to Charleston right before my twelfth birthday to get some work, and hoped I would meet up with them again.

They nodded and asked more questions. When we left, I told them, "Mama has been telling me for a long time that Africans are just as good as anybody else. She's taken me to church so I could hear preaching, and to baptisms and quarterly meetings. But she also taught me the value of hard work and obedience to the McKees, other white people and black grownups as well."

Nodding and smiling, the one who had read to me spoke. "You'll be fine in Charleston. You got a good head on you, Robert. Make your Mama proud."

FOUR
Robert

"Mama, do I have a brother?" I nearly tripped as I rushed back to the cabin from the McKee's home, where I had overheard a conversation between Elizabeth McKee and her mother.

Mama looked puzzled before she slowly nodded. "Yes, Robert. You do. I had a son twenty-one years ago. Why are you asking me now?"

I told her what Elizabeth and her mother said. I felt resentful that they knew and I didn't. I believed that, at ten years of age, I should be included in adult conversations.

"Where is he, Mama? I want to know him."

She exhaled a tired breath and sat down, folding her hands together in her lap. "Son, I lost him early on. He was sold to a planter in Mississippi when he was just a few months old."

I definitely did not expect that answer. "Why didn't you tell me? Did you name him?"

"Of course I did. His name is Larry Polite. I don't know if he is even alive today. I have no way to find out." Her voice cracked as she softly spoke. "I should have told you about him, but it is still too painful for me to talk about."

"Is his daddy my father? I don't even know who my daddy is! I want to know!"

Tears misted in Mama's eyes and I quickly regretted my outburst. She took a step forward and put her finger under my chin to raise my head. "Son, I will tell you when the time is right. He is not in our lives, and I don't believe that information would change your life now."

My youthful emotions fought against my better judgment. I wanted to shout out terrible things to her, but common sense overcame my anger. She began rubbing my back and I allowed her to comfort me.

Mama wiped a tear from her eye. Very slowly and quietly, she said, "It was like the hurt was so deep I couldn't let it out of me. I couldn't find the words to describe it."

I nodded and looked down, avoiding her eyes.

"Robert, we all choose how we think, how we speak, and how we treat others. Everyone has a good heart and an evil heart. Each of us must choose which one we'll feed."

I struggled to fight back sorrowful tears as they rolled down my cheeks. Slowly, she released me.

"To find your peace, you must fill your heart with love and hope. Be a forgiving person, and you will discover your own truth." She smiled, wiping my face with a wet towel. "Why don't we go gather some eggs, and I'll fix something special for you."

My eleven years of childhood were spent in Beaufort, where 83% of the population was made up of slaves. A Beaufort ordinance required all enslaved people to be in their quarters after sundown, unless they were in the company of their owners. There was a bronze bell on top of the church that rang every night to signal the beginning of the black curfew. I hated its sound and especially resented that when I was outside playing with my white friends, I had to stop and go indoors when the bell rang. My rebellious nature occasionally took over and I refused to go inside. I was even arrested several times. Mr. McKee got me released from jail and warned me not to repeat this offense. But I did, knowing he would spring me again.

When I left for my new life in Charleston, I was strong, nervous, and quite excited. I was eager to learn and discover new things. Master McKee, our aging driver, Uncle George, and I climbed aboard the horse-drawn carriage carrying enough luggage to see me through many months and even years. Before Missus McKee went shopping for me, I had almost no clothes. Now I had too many! She wisely bought them a little large so I could grow into them.

"But I will see you again during this time away, right? And my mama too? I am already missing her and my friends in Beaufort."

"Yes, Robert. We'll check on you, and I'll make sure that you will see Lydia," smiled Mr. McKee.

Looking back, I think he knew they were sending me into a new world to make a difference. He and Mama and Missus McKee had prepared me in the best way they could, even though I lived under their bondage. They socialized me, taught me proper English and excellent manners, and provided me the protection and care a father is expected to give. They also shaped my attitudes and habits, and gave me skills and values that served me into manhood. I am very grateful that I can finally recognize that now.

Mr. McKee did not set me free, but he taught me what I needed to know to eventually succeed.

For more than five years, I lived in a cabin in Charleston, just behind Eliza Ancrum's plantation house. When we arrived, Mr. McKee and Uncle George stayed with me for two weeks to show me around. My master helped me get my first job in Charleston as a waiter in the Planters

Hotel. I was paid $5.00 a month, and he let me keep $1.00. I was on my way.

I began to make new friends. I was told that the black population numbered nearly 32,000 when I arrived. Because of its diverse economy, this city offered a broad range of opportunities, as opposed to Beaufort. The census of 1850 did not list a single free Negro in Beaufort County. Charleston did have a free Negro underclass of tradesmen and property owners. They traveled at liberty throughout the city, paid taxes and enjoyed many rights. I heard about the right to rent themselves out and be allowed to work. I was very interested in learning more.

Charleston had become a vigorous manufacturing center, and I met free slaves with relatively independent lifestyles. I continued to learn more about Frederick Douglass, who had become my champion, even though I couldn't read his papers. That made me more determined to learn to read.

In the educational field, Charleston was better established than many other places. There was a system of free schools for free blacks, run by free black men and women. One person working with these schools was Francis Cardozo, who eventually became one of my mentors. He taught in one of those schools, and would become a lifelong friend.

After working for a time as a waiter, I was offered another job: lamplighter for The Charleston Gas Light Company. In 1851, gas lamps were still relatively new to the city. My job was to clean the globes and remove soot from the jets in the morning and light the lamps in the evening. I liked this work because it gave me much more independence, and I didn't have to worry about keeping demanding dinner customers happy.

When I was almost fourteen, I began to actively look for work on the docks. Since I was completely comfortable around the water, I took advantage of that during my Christmas visit to Beaufort. I asked Mr. McKee if I could work at the docks in Charleston, and assured him how well I was already trained, due to his tutelage. He interceded and acquired a position for me as a stevedore, loading and unloading cargo from the numerous ships entering the port. Being the curious person that I am, I enjoyed working with free blacks, enslaved blacks, and white immigrants. As others had predicted, I soon developed my own ideas and took advantage of opportunities offered to me during this time.

After only a year on the docks, I was promoted to supervisor and oversaw men twice my age. Then I had the good fortune of meeting Mr. John Simmons, who immediately employed me as a rigger. He taught me how to make rope lines to attach the boat sails together, and honed my skills to turn into an expert rigger.

Mr. Simmons and I became mutually respectful friends. In the summer, he used me as a sailor and a pilot on coastal vessels. He was the man who elevated my position to wheelman, or boat pilot. He told me that as a slave, I could not be entitled "Captain." I knew that, yet I was doing the work of a captain. As a wheelman, I traveled through Georgia and northern Florida. I am grateful to this kind man who taught me so much and gave me the privilege of his time and friendship.

I also attended several churches and participated in an organization called the Seven Societies of Blacks. That group may have assembled in violation of the laws of South Carolina. I mingled with slaves and free blacks at the meetings. These societies were primarily formed "to help one another in sickness and distress," but the subject of freedom was openly discussed. We had to be careful because we didn't fully trust the other members. As in church, we prayed constantly for the "day of our deliverance." I was thriving, listening and learning.

My pay had increased and I continued to give the majority to Master McKee. Still, he increased the amount I could keep. I also bought and sold fruit from the docks, so I was able to save a little money. The physical, economic, social and cultural advantages of Charleston, and its black presence and diverse population, opened this city as fertile ground for me. I slowly began to build a career, laying the foundation for my own family one day. Ultimately, I started my research, which led to my daring plan of escape from slavery.

FIVE

Hannah

Robert and I laughed easily during the Sundays we spent together. We had been seeing each other for over a year now, and he kept his word about searching for a way to live together if we ever got married.

This afternoon we're passing time simply by sitting on the dock and looking out over the horizon. Two large pelicans were keeping watch over us from the pillars. They rose together, circled lazily and then soared higher. One of them folded his wings and plunged straight down into the water. Several long moments passed before he emerged with a fish. He threw back his head and swallowed it whole.

"Wow! That was a lesson in perseverance," I declared, rolling my eyes good-naturedly. Robert stroked my hair and kissed the top of my head.

I sighed softly. "Cap, I've been thinking that if we ever do get married, what would happen to our children? Would they belong to Master Kingsman, like my girls do already? Is there no other option?"

His bushy eyebrows shot up. "Sugar, lean back, inhale slowly and just taste the salty air."

I did and laughed. He always found a way to amuse me during our serious discussions.

"You know that I've saved some money. Maybe Mr. McKee will let me buy you and your girls. That would keep us together."

"Until they trade one of us off. Then what happens?" Frowning, I reached for his hand.

"Mr. McKee is coming to Charleston next weekend. I'm planning to make a direct appeal to him, and I've practiced my defense well," he said somberly. "Let not your heart be troubled," he grinned.

In my mind I was cheering, but anyone watching me wouldn't see that.

But knowing Robert, I realized he would perform well.

Robert and Mr. McKee had a long and successful conversation about our dilemma. Robert tried to remember all the details to share with me, but I'm sure some of them escaped him.

"Did he agree to give us permission to marry?" I was impatient to know the final decision.

"His exact words were: 'I'm not opposed to your idea, Robert. But you'll also have to get Kingman's permission. And he's a hard man, as you know.'"

"And you told him about how white men and women get married and live in the same house, just like free black men and women do? So why should enslaved persons have to live separately in quarters provided by their respective masters?"

"Yes dear, I did. And I said we aren't willing to settle for that."

I nodded, barely able to speak due to the lump forming inside me. At least he had received Mr. McKee's approval! The next step was getting Mr. Kingman's permission, which would be more difficult.

"Cap, it's in their best interest, and they know it. It helps the morale of their slaves and even adds to the owner's wealth, because any children of enslaved women are the master's property. And it keeps the male slaves from running away."

Robert wrapped his arms around me. "You are a clever lady, my lovely Hannah, and I've come up with another plan to get us Kingman's permission."

I jumped up. "What is it?"

"I will offer to pay him $5.00 per month, and remind him how responsible and reliable we are, and deserving of this unique relationship. I'll ask him to allow us to live together in our own place that we'll rent somewhere. I'm earning $16.00 monthly, plus what I sell to the seamen from the fruits and vegetables I purchase. How can he deny us permission?"

I frowned at him. "He'll want me to pay him something as well."

"Yes. I've already thought of that. How about $5.00 a month? And I'll ask Mr. McKee to allow me to work extra and keep everything over the $15 he takes from my salary."

I laughed gleefully. Would it be possible to persuade both owners?

It was! And I'm convinced he won them over because Robert was persuasive, articulate and unique with his human relations skills. I asked him to give me the details.

He told me that he approached Mr. Kingsman and asked for his permission for us to marry.

"You do know, Smalls, that by law, slaves cannot legally marry, don't you?" Kingsman was taken aback by the unusual proposal.

"Yes, Sir, Master Kingsman. But some owners have granted permission for an *unofficial marriage*, after which we would be able to live together."

He looked beyond me and scratched his chin. "What can you offer to entice me?"

I smiled at him and looked him in the eye. "I can pay you $5.00 per month, and I'll take care of Hannah and get us a place to live as a family."

After a long moment, he agreed. "I'll be expecting that payment at the first of each month."

"Yes, Sir, Master Kingsman. I am much obliged. Thank you, Sir."

"I'm so proud of you, Robert! The Lord was with us. Let's plan our wedding in Beaufort for this upcoming Christmas Eve." We raised our eyes upward. The bright sun heated our skin. We watched as an egret rose from the grasses, its long wings shining like a shield of white against the deep blue of the sky.

Our wedding was perfect, and exactly what we wanted. We got married on Christmas Eve, 1856. The McKees wanted the ceremony to be in their new home on Carteret and Bay. This house was purchased the year Robert went to Charleston to work. Dear Uncle George picked us up in Charleston and drove us to Beaufort. And most importantly, he assumed the role of my father and gave me away.

We stood under a magnolia tree in the McKee's back yard, looking into the eyes of Rev. Mansfield French and enjoying the bells of St. Helena Episcopal Church. Mr. McKee asked our Methodist preacher to officiate.

Rev. French smiled at us, delighted by our audacity and by the diversity of people surrounding us that afternoon. "It is God's will," he spoke softly.

Robert's mother, Lydia, presided over the entire affair, as well she should. She, with the help of Mr. McKee's staff, chose, organized, and prepared all the food. She looked beautiful in a light purple sheer gown she had sewn. Lydia also made my wedding gown, from pieces of material she had left over from sewing Missus McKee's gowns.

I cried when I learned that Mr. McKee was able to persuade Mr. Kingsman to allow my mother, Sadie, and my daughters, Charlotte and Clara, to attend. When Rev. French told me he had never witnessed a white family host a wedding for a slave, I smiled joyfully. "Can you see the mutual affection we have for the McKee family?"

Henry and Jane McKee and their family shared in our festivities, especially their daughter Elizabeth, now seventeen, and eleven-year-old William. They each had a small, but special, part in the ceremony. Many of our friends, both white and black, joined us.

After our vows, Rev. French nodded to my mother. She stood, solemn and motivated, and reclaimed a short-handled broom from under her chair. Carrying it to Rev. French, she paused, turned to Robert and me, and looked intently into our eyes.

Lifting up the broom, Sadie waved it three times. Her lips moved slowly and silently above our heads. I believe she was praying. Suddenly, in one motion, she arranged it on the ground in front of us, and then gave us her big smile. She nodded once, and Robert took my hand. Mama nodded again, and we jumped over the broom together, crying out shouts of joy! Applause and laughter exploded. Rev. French then pronounced us man and wife.

It was a magical ceremony—the most perfect day. We shared both laughter and tears with our guests throughout the evening.

We dined on steamed baby-back ribs, pulled pork and corn on the cob, great bowls of baked beans, fish cooked in a big iron pot on the beach, and Lydia's loaves of just-baked bread. I don't know how it all came together at the perfect time, but it did. The McKees paid for everything as their wedding gift to us.

We ate, sang, danced and lit firecrackers until the dawn of Christmas Day.

"Baby, this is the beginning of your role as head of the family," I whispered to him. "You will carry that honor well, and we'll be blessed by your guidance."

"Hannah dear, this is the happiest moment of my life. I will make you and our family proud." I pulled him close and kissed him, unable to speak. He continued, "And one day we'll add to this family, God willing."

We returned to Charleston and moved into a little two-room apartment above a livery stable on East Bay Street. In exchange for Robert's cleaning out the stalls, we lived there rent free, and saved that money. Robert insisted we invest it into his business enterprise: a small neighborhood shop. Friends gave us furniture, hardware, and whatever else we needed. We knew we were fortunate, and entered into our marriage with confidence and hope.

SIX

Elizabeth

From all accounts, my parents spent the first several years after their marriage as happily as they could. They lived in Charleston and worked on building a life together, in spite of not being free. Fortunately, I came into their lives two years later, on February 12, 1858. They told me that my birth brought them great joy, and together they chose my name: Elizabeth Lydia. Elizabeth is Daddy's dear childhood friend (the daughter of his owner) with whom he grew up during his twelve years of childhood in Beaufort. And Lydia, who they both love, is his mother's name. They told me they wanted to honor them both.

It wasn't long before my father became deeply concerned that our family might be separated by others, and according to my mother, he was desperate to find a way to keep us together. By law, I became the property of Mr. Kingsman, just as my mother was. I believe Mr. Kingsman was pleased by my birth, knowing that other children would probably come along. Daddy condemned those ownership norms and told others that after I was born, he became concerned about his family's freedom.

Then my parents came up with an even better strategy! First, Daddy asked to speak with his owner, Mr. McKee, knowing he would need his permission for his drastic proposal. He would tell him that he was now in an excellent situation to make more money, reminding him how frugal he'd been over the past year, and that Mama was also working and making money.

My parents discussed this together before Daddy went to Mr. McKee.

"Will he understand, Cap? We both know that the law is interpreted by powerful white men," Hannah told him. He knew she could speak great pearls of wisdom using only a few words.

He took several moments to answer. "Yes, Sugar, but this time I feel that the Lord will help us prevail."

During Mr. McKee's next visit to Charleston, he approached him.

"Mas' McKee, what do you think about me purchasing Hannah and little Lizzie from Mr. Kingsman?" At this point in time, the idea of an enslaved person owning another slave had not been recognized in either practice or legislature.

To their enormous relief, Daddy's owner readily agreed to his unusual request. He had nothing to lose, because he owned my Daddy and everything he had. Our family often mentioned that Mr. McKee's consent was just another loving favor he was prepared to give us.

Now my Daddy had to ask Master Kingsman to allow him to purchase Mama and me. He knew this was an "illegal" request, but in typical Robert Smalls fashion, he marched right in.

"Mas' Kingsman, you know that what I'm proposing is commercially beneficial to you, as well as profitable. You know I'm responsible and I keep my word. My wife and I have kept up with the payments to you that we negotiated in the marriage agreement."

Mr. Kingsman nodded in agreement. "And what is your price for the sale of your purchase?" he inquired.

My father hadn't thought that far. "Sir, please tell me," he said, managing to keep his expression blank.

Mr. Kingsman grunted. "I will sell your wife and your daughter to you for $800."

According to my parents' version of the story, Daddy bowed slightly and said, "Mas' Kingsman, my wife and I have $100 saved up, and we will give this to you as a down payment. We can give you the rest later."

It was a gentlemen's agreement, settled with a handshake. Both of them knew how serious and trusting this needed to be. Not many slaves could make that statement or that agreement. This deal involved several parties. Kingsman had contracted to sell his two slaves to Robert Smalls. Mr. McKee had contracted to permit my father to own us. My parents had committed to pay a specified price over an indefinite period of time. I believe it's a tribute to everyone involved in this difficult, partly commercial/partly familiar agreement.

My parents told me that for the next three years they saved everything they could. They fully intended to follow through on their obligation. Mama worked in a different hotel with a higher salary, and also laundered sailors' shirts while they were docked in Charleston. Daddy bought and sold fruits and vegetables on the waterfront. By 1861, they had saved up the $700 they owed Mr. Kingsman. During this time, my father worked hard to understand maps, channels, tides and currents. Amazingly, he did all of this without being able to read.

My father quickly became an expert boatman. They say that few men along the South Carolina coastal waters could handle a boat like Robert Smalls.

I was happy to experience, and appreciate, the ideal match my parents appeared to be. Through good times and difficult times, through danger and sadness, they worked together. They showed me what family happiness looked like.

~

My parents were believers and attended church services whenever they could. Charleston is a city of many churches, and experienced a large increase in black church membership between 1830 and 1860. The galleries of Charleston's white Baptist and Methodist churches were filled with black members. The Presbyterians and Episcopalians had fewer black members, but reached out to the children through their Sunday schools. And on the plantations, white planters invited blacks to their churches, believing that their Christian duty was to evangelize.

We attended church wherever we were: Beaufort, Charleston and on the plantation. I particularly enjoyed going to the African Church in Charleston, called the AME (African Methodist Episcopal) Church. Their preachers went to Philadelphia to be trained and ordained by Bishop Richard Allen. This particular church had an interesting history that heartened me.

When we were in Beaufort, we attended Beaufort Baptist. Reverend Richard Fuller was a powerful teacher, and loved watching his congregation enter the sanctuary each Sunday. Businessmen and planters entered first, filling the pews on the main floor. Next came the slaves and servants, who entered into the church, singing and clapping and swaying as they made their way up to the balcony seats.

The first time my family took me to Beaufort Baptist, I was astounded. "Are they singing these songs for us?" I asked Daddy.

He nodded and gave me a mischievous grin. "For us, for themselves, for God. This is a happy occasion where we all come together as sisters and brothers in Christ."

The procession slowed when we entered the church, two and three abreast. Clinging to Mama's hand, I walked with them as we wound our way to the front of the sanctuary, passing right in front of Reverend Fuller, who stood at the altar smiling broadly. We moved to the center aisle, still swaying, clapping and singing, and only paused when we reached the back of the church. Then we climbed up the stairs to the gallery, where we found a place to watch the activities.

Their welcome felt sincere and the message was long but quite satisfying. I really enjoyed the music, and rocked side-to-side with my parents and the others. We continued singing, even more joyously. A warm feeling filled my heart. After the long service, the white members shared a feast with the blacks. It seemed almost magical and perfect.

But a question was running through my mind. "Daddy, are these the same people who whip our slave brothers and sisters?"

Daddy paused several seconds before bending over to whisper in my ear. "Lizzie, they are. But here we learn how God loves the slaves and how we should live. We learn about forgiveness too. Listen closely to the preacher's words."

I waited for answers and I heard them. "Keep everyone close and enclose them in the language and fervor of righteousness. God's own word says He loves each and every one of us. He gives each of us an ordained place in His Kingdom, which is created of ivory (here he looked at the white families) and created of ebony." At this point his eyes lifted up to the faces of the black congregation in the gallery.

He began and ended with his big black Bible. "This is the word of God," he preached. "Thanks be to God," answered all the people. The other churches were similar, but I particularly liked this one in Beaufort. It made Sunday a very special time for me and so many others.

SEVEN

Hannah

The firing on Fort Sumter on April 12, 1861, completely interrupted our life plans. None of us knew it then, but this attack marked the first shot fired in the Civil War. Robert was assigned to navigate *The CSS Planter*, a lightly-armed Confederate military transport under Charleston's District Commander, Brigadier General Roswell S. Ripley. Built in Charleston in 1860, this ship was fitted with two cannons, designated as an "armed dispatch boat," and leased to Confederate engineers.

Robert's duties were to survey the waterways, deliver dispatches, troops and supplies, and lay mines when necessary. Because he now piloted *The Planter* throughout Charleston, Georgia and the Florida coasts, he was often away from me, and that was hard on our little family.

We gave thanks and glory to God for the gift of a baby son, who we named Robert Smalls, Jr. His pet name was Beauregard, and he came into our lives in February of 1861, just two months before the outbreak of the war. His birth was celebrated, but we had no idea what would follow. There was no advance warning that it would be war.

Union troops, under the command of Major Robert Anderson, had occupied Fort Sumter since the day after Christmas of 1860. He recognized how vulnerable his troops were across the harbor at Fort Moultrie, especially since South Carolina had seceded from the Union just two days before.

So we weren't completely surprised that night when the Citadel boys began firing on the fort. We watched the attack on Fort Sumter from the docks, and witnessed the celebrations that followed in the streets of Charleston. Charleston's wealthiest observed it all from their mansion windows and verandas, just behind us on the Battery.

Robert and I heard the shots from our room and ran down to the waterfront. We sat with others for a couple of hours, watching the explosions over the fort. Their brilliant reflections illuminating the water were astonishing. It didn't appear that the Union men were returning fire. But just after dawn they struck back.

We looked across the harbor and could make out the line of federal blockade ships in the outer harbor, about seven miles away.

"What are they doing for food over there?" I wondered aloud. We'd been told that when President Lincoln took office in March, the Union troops stationed at the fort were in great need of food and other provisions.

Robert was physically exhausted, and his face had become pinched and thin. "In spite of the Confederates' orders, the federal troops living at Fort Sumter refused to surrender. *The Planter* took some indispensable supplies to them. This includes the food and other necessary effects I see when we deliver them."

"Oh Cap, watching the Confederates rejoice at their victory is so disturbing to the black community. How do you feel about this?" I asked fearfully, nursing our son with one arm as I warmed up the soup.

"It troubles me greatly, Sugar." His face took on a grim expression. "It's a bad sign for our future."

I was edgy and sleepless as well. "Negotiations have failed. Some Southern states wanting to keep slavery, like South Carolina, have broken from the Union," I said. "Is this just the beginning of many months of evil and bloodshed?" I didn't tell him that I had a bad feeling in my bones.

⁓

The Planter became a warship for the Confederate States of America. Her owner, Mr. Ferguson, was encouraged to lease it to the new Confederacy. *The Planter* had started as a cotton steamer. Just one hundred forty-seven feet long and thirty feet wide, she was considered a fine boat. She was built on a live-oak frame with red cedar boards, two engines and a side paddle-wheel. Although she had carried fourteen hundred bales of cotton, she would now move men—a thousand at a time. She could also carry munitions, which seemed to be her primary purpose.

She was a fast boat and agile as well. She could reverse course immediately when the wheels were turned in opposite directions. Mr. Ferguson wanted to pilot her, but the Confederacy removed him for another pilot and kept the crew. They knew my Robert was an important part of the crew, and he stayed on to the end.

Robert's new captain, Captain Relyea, was a man who loved to dress stylishly. Robert said he was quite impressed with himself, showing off his uniform whenever he could, even off the boat. He had a habit of leaning against the cabin window and crossing his arms over his chest, which gave him a look of arrogance.

My husband was delighted to be kept on as helmsman and was certain he knew the waters from Charleston to Savannah and beyond better than any other pilot. The low country's tides and marshes were all familiar, and he skillfully slid *The Planter* over shallow spots and shoehorned it down narrow creeks. He gained the trust of every member of the crew, including the Captain.

Their assignments took them to Port Royal and even to Beaufort, where he could briefly visit his mother Lydia. She always sent something she'd cooked back with him, and a little treat for her darling grandbabies, Lizzie and Beauregard.

On those journeys, Robert told me he often reflected on his feelings about working for the Confederates. I knew that really bothered him, because he realized that even though his crew worked together so well, their work was reinforcing bondage.

Shortly after we had that conversation, we attended the Sunday service at the Baptist Church and listened closely to the preacher's message. I tried to remember as much as I could, but the main point that stuck with me was: "The Northerners believe that slavery is a sin and must be abolished. The Southerners believe it's a scriptural institution. It is the duty of religious bodies to define their position in this challenge."

"Oh Baby," he whispered to me, "I'm working for the Confederates and want to be working for God. How did this happen?"

And then the war intensified. In July of 1861, a Confederate victory at the Battle of Bull Run near Manassas made many in Washington, D.C., understand that the fighting wouldn't end soon.

Robert and some of his friends sat with us one Sunday evening and we discussed this.

"Washington is concerned that slave labor is providing the South with an advantage. So they just authorized what they call the first 'Confiscation Act.' Now the Union can seize any slaves helping in the rebellion." Robert opened the meeting with this unusual statement.

I jumped in. "What does that mean?" I waited for him to continue.

Robert heard about this from others in the shipping industry. "The way I understand it is that slaves seized by the Union are no longer obligated to their former masters, but they aren't emancipated. They will be called 'contraband.'"

A crew member added, "They should be given their freedom. But remember the Dred Scott decision… that people with African background, slaves or free, can never be citizens of America."

I imagined people were discussing these issues all over the country. Even President Lincoln's cabinet argued about how to respond. President Lincoln wanted to preserve the Union, and this could only come about by placating the slave states that had not seceded.

"Well, I heard that President Lincoln wanted to end slavery by sending all the blacks out of the country to Africa or somewhere else," I said, having overheard a conversation at the hotel.

So it went on and on. Robert attended meetings with his groups, and continued to learn about Frederick Douglass. "Frederick argues that emancipation should be a major aim of the war and that would help the Union succeed. He wrote: *The very stomach of this rebellion is the Negro in the form of a slave.*"

Our future would remain unclear for some time yet. But we had learned to live day by day, and to do the best we could.

Things began to change at the end of the year. Through several reliable sources, we learned that the U.S Navy had assembled a large armada to head south. The plan was to capture a deep-water harbor to serve as a fuel and provisioning depot for the ships blockading the coasts of South Carolina, Georgia and Florida.

The man in charge of the armada was Commander Samuel Francis Du Pont. Their destination was the Port Royal Sound, near Beaufort. (Most of the information about this incident came from Robert's mother, Lydia, during his visits with her). This sound was a deep natural harbor that would provide the Union with the supply depot it needed. But in order to capture Port Royal Sound, the Union would have to get through two Confederate forts—Fort Walker and Fort Beauregard. These forts were recently constructed by slave workers in case of an attack by Union forces.

Du Pont's flagship, the *Wabash,* and twenty-five other ships, anchored off Port Royal on November 4, 1861. Three days later, they entered the inlet with Fort Beauregard on the right and Fort Walker on the left. The ships engaged in a fury of cannon fire that lasted into the early afternoon. They then turned around and bombed each fort again. Five hours later, the Confederates departed. The battle had been short, and the casualties were few. Du Pont had captured the harbor the Union desperately needed. Port Royal was now under Union control-the first major Union naval victory of the war.

Because the approach of the large armada frightened the Confederates, Charleston's General Ripley warned the people of Beaufort to evacuate. The families rushed to pack their belongings and bury family silver and other valuables. The slaves did most of the work, but then refused to leave themselves. When the Union troops arrived and asked about the exodus, the slaves told them that their masters had run away because they feared a slave revolt.

Lydia and most of Henry McKee's one hundred slaves remained behind. A few planters showed concern for the slaves who remained behind. Some were Union sympathizers and allowed the slaves to stay and work the needed crops instead of the cotton. Other planters did what they could to protect the town's assets from falling into the Union's hands. Henry McKee hid barrels of gunpowder before he and his men departed.

With their masters gone and the Union soldiers not arriving immediately at Beaufort, the slaves, free from their captors for the first time, ransacked homes. They took clothing, food and whatever else they wanted or needed for their families. Some white residents even returned during the chaos in Beaufort to burn their valuable Sea Island cotton so the Union could not profit from it. Others destroyed armaments at the arsenal. They reported that all the houses had been ransacked. The churches were robbed of valuable items that were stock piled in them for safe keeping. In addition, some Union soldiers plundered abandoned plantations on Hilton Head and other islands. They took what they wanted and destroyed the rest.

Generals Sherman and Du Pont were furious and issued orders forbidding military men to enter private homes. Du Pont even stopped unauthorized boats on their way to various islands. These commanders did not know what to do with all the slaves who remained. Trying to entice the planters to return, they posted a proclamation in newspapers addressed to the people of South Carolina. "Return to your homes and your slaves. We have no intention of harming them or your properties."

The South Carolinians ignored the notices. Military officers went by boat to Beaufort, carrying a flag of truce. Confederates were willing to talk to them, but not willing to deliver the proclamation on behalf of the Union.

The effort to bring back the wealthy residents failed. They did not return. The Union's arrival had shattered the prosperous lives they'd been living. Lydia told us that Beaufort, the first town captured by the Union, had changed overnight. The planters had lost everything. Some would never return; others tried for years after the war to reclaim their homes and property. But they would never again hold the power they held before the war.

EIGHT

Lydia and Hannah

The city of Charleston quickly learned about the war that started in Beaufort, South Carolina. Because Robert knew I was basically alone, he made sure to come by to visit me.

"Mama, I'm happy that you are safe and have food. Uncle George will continue to care for you and the others. But it's so upsetting to see that Beaufort has suffered all this damage." He couldn't stop hugging me.

"Son, I hear that the Union forces are close to Charleston. Do you think they'll ransack that city as well?"

He took a few moments to think about his answer. "I don't know, Mama. But I am relieved that you are in Union territory at least. Their protection keeps you safer."

"Oh Robert, have you heard what the Union is saying about enslaved people?"

"What, Mama?"

"They say we are now called 'contrabands' and basically free. This includes all the slaves from Beaufort."

"Yes, we heard. That's because you are under Union control." He leaned against me, overcome with emotion. "And my family and I are still enslaved."

I put a finger under his chin and raised his head. My palm rested gently on his cheek. "Son, what does that 'freedom' mean to me? We are now weak and suffering, with a new sense of hopelessness. I believe our hard lives will get harder."

"Then you'll come with me to Charleston. I won't let you suffer."

I let him go, knowing he would come for me. Realizing that my grandchildren were in a better location than I, comforted my soul. My boy Robert is a good man, and I am proud of him.

⁓

No attack was made on Charleston, but the city endured another tragedy. In December, a horrific fire raged through the city, leaving destruction that burned 145 acres. About six hundred homes burned. So did churches and other buildings. Indeed, Charleston looked like it had gone through a war.

The city was suffering. Robert and Hannah managed because they had access to supplies. Other slaves were not so lucky. The North hated the Confederates and would love to capture their city, but no attack came during the winter.

During this time, my son and his friends began planning their escape. Of course I did not know about this until later, but it kept Robert and Hannah busy and hopeful.

Hannah was the one who told me the story. She had known that Robert longed to escape but didn't realize that he had been formulating a plan and intended to execute it. When he finally shared it with her, she was shocked.

"Oh Baby, why have you left me out of this escape planning?" Her eyes were confused.

"Hannah, I needed to thoroughly go over this in my mind and have it ready to explain before I involved you."

Hannah sat down on the bed and hugged her elbows to her body. A little more calmly, she replied, "I know that life doesn't give us guarantees; we only have dreams. But what kind of heartache will we feel when this dream is broken?"

"You must believe and trust in me, dear Hannah. I wouldn't expose you and our children to something I thought would fail."

Her eyes widened as his words sank in.

"When will this happen?" she asked.

"Soon. One night when *The Planter* is docked and the officers leave to spend time with their families. We have to be ready to gather what we need and to escape at a moment's notice."

"Cap, have you even discussed this with the crew yet?

He reached for her hands. "No, Sugar. I wanted to talk to you first."

She smiled and softly answered, "Thank you, Baby."

He continued, "You see, there is a part of me that wants to leave you and the children here. We may all be killed or kill ourselves, so logically you women and children should stay behind. If we make it, I will return for you."

Hannah felt the lump forming in her throat as tears welled in her eyes. She rose to retrieve her black Bible from our room. "Let me read to you the words of Ruth," she said.

Hannah's supervisor at the hotel was slowly teaching her to read. She was uncomfortable picking out words, but wanted to study the Bible so she practiced whenever she could. The Bible gave her comfort, and she memorized her favorite verses, which she loved to share.

With her sweet voice, she began. "Where you go, I will go and where you stay, I will stay. Your people will be my people, and your God my God. *Ruth 1, Chapter* 16."

Robert bowed his head, and when he looked up at her, his eyes were misty. "Oh beloved woman, your love for me is deep and powerful, just as you are. I am indeed a blessed man."

Suddenly she pointed to the window. "Cap, look outside. Just see how the sky has turned the color of ripe peaches. Surely this is a sign that God is with us."

So it was decided. We would take our family. We would live together or perish together.

Several days later Robert gathered the crew of *The Planter* in their two-room quarters above the horse stable on East Bay Street. He explained the plan, and they worked out the details. He turned to Hannah and asked her opinion about leaving the women and children behind. In a steady voice she repeated what she had told him earlier. But she added another verse, declaring "I will go, and where you die, I will die." The men nodded solemnly. Robert asked them to think seriously about this, and if they decided to take their women and children, not to give them any details. "Tell them only that they will pay a visit to the steamer one evening soon."

~

On Monday, May 12, 1862, Robert and his crew tied *The Planter* to the southern dock after they finished two weeks of supply duty. The officers—Captain C. J. Relyea, pilot Samuel H. Smith, and engineer E. Zerich Pitcher—took advantage of the completion of this grueling work to spend the night ashore with their families. (These officers were violating military orders by staying onshore overnight). Just before the officers left the boat, Robert asked Captain Relyea if the crew's families could have a brief visit, which was occasionally allowed by boat captains.

"Certainly, Smalls. Just make sure they depart before curfew." He grabbed his bag, and left. Robert noticed he departed without his Captain's jacket. It was left hanging on its hook: an advantageous omen for sure.

During the previous weeks, Union forces had placed a blockade in the Charleston harbor, to prevent Confederate forces from getting out to the Atlantic Ocean and engaging in foreign trade.

First mate Hancock suddenly announced he would sleep on the steamer that night. Robert bided his time, going about his routine task, until he could speak quietly to Hancock.

"We cannot abandon our plans now. I will have to lock you up in your room if you stay onboard. You may leave now and go ashore, but I need your word of honor that you will tell no one what we are planning."

Hancock irritably said he would leave the ship after all and tell no one.

A few minutes later two deckhands announced they had changed their minds, and wanted off as well. Robert let them go. "I understand, Jones and Gibbs, but like with Hancock, you must swear to secrecy. You will not betray your mates and sabotage our mission."

For a while, the rest of the crew was concerned that one of these men would divulge our plans. Fortunately, at the last moment, three other men who were initially interested, came aboard the steamer. Now they would have enough hands to operate the vessel.

It was time to execute the prepared plan. Robert gave them last minute instructions.

"Crew, the Captain told me the Confederate guard boat that monitors the entrance to the harbor is temporarily out of commission. Because of this, I heard that Charleston will be placed under martial law tomorrow in anticipation of a Union attack."

He watched their faces to read their reactions. "This is why I have chosen tonight for the escape," he continued. The men concurred.

As their women arrived, the men shared the plan with them. Mrs. Lavinia Wilson was owned by a cashier at a Charleston Bank, and Anna White was her relative. They all believed they had been invited for a visit to the ship, but after only a few moments, they became suspicious.

"It's almost curfew time. We should leave," Anna announced timidly.

Robert gathered them around him and spoke. The women met the news with concern, alarm and fear. They suddenly realized the magnitude of this escape plot. Several began to weep, others put their heads in their hands and moaned softly. A few, led by Hannah, begged God for help and safety.

Robert had frightened them, yet with the tenacity of a bulldog, he got their attention. He admitted that if the attempt failed, they would be shot or hanged. He told them if they were attacked, they would hold hands and jump overboard to drown themselves.

"But we will be successful, I believe. There is no turning back. We have refused to go back to slavery. You will free your children and yourselves. We must do this for our people!" There was silence now. Their heads nodded in agreement.

Nevertheless, it took a while to calm everyone. We locked the women in the stateroom and threated to kill anyone who made a noise. Fortunately, Hannah was able to soothe them with Bible stories and prayer during the time the men prepared to move them and the children to a nearby vessel.

At some point, three crew members pretended to escort the family members back home, but they circled around and hid them aboard another steamer docked at the North Atlantic wharf. Around 3:00 a.m. on May 13, 1862, Robert, the women and children, and seven of the eight enslaved crewmen carried out their previously planned escape.

NINE

Robert

I put on Captain Relyea's floppy straw hat, partly to cover my face, but mostly to give myself a sense of authority. Tonight, I will be the Captain. The moment I saw Captain Relyea hang his gold-trimmed Captain's jacket on the hook, I knew this was a blessing from God: one that began the day my crewman friend John noticed that I was about the same size as Captain Relyea.

"If you wore his clothes, you could pass for him from a distance."

I played along, posed at the wheel in his jacket and even walked around with a limp. We both laughed, but I tucked that memory away. When I told Hannah later, she chuckled and said I was very bold and maybe a little crazy. The jacket fit me well, and when I crossed my arms at the wheel, as he often does, I felt like a captain.

I knew that by leaving the wharf in the early hours we would pass Fort Sumter at first light. That was vital. If we arrived any earlier, those on guard might wonder why we were traveling in the dark. And if we left later, someone on shore might notice there were no white officers on board.

Around 3 a.m., my crew prepared to leave, and added more wood to the fires to heat up the boilers. Once there was enough steam, we were ready to leave. The wind had picked up unexpectedly. I realized this would carry smoke over the city, probably drawing attention to the wharf.

Only five months ago, Charleston had one of the worst fires in its history. It destroyed much of the city, so the residents had become watchful of smoke.

Minutes ticked by and we all braced for trouble, but nothing happened. When the fog began to thin, I ordered two flags to be raised. One was the official Confederate flag, known as the Stars and Bars, and the second was South Carolina's blue and white state flag, with its Palmetto tree and a crescent. This was necessary to preserve our cover as a Confederate vessel.

Allston, serving as wheelman, and I moved to the pilothouse of *The Planter*. The ship slowly backed away from the wharf, using the whistles to signal it was preparing to begin a normal day's business.

"Dear God, please steer us with Your hands, not mine. Let me reach my family and bring them onboard," I prayed, noticing my hands were trembling as I raised them up to the heavens.

Stopping quickly at the North Atlantic dock, we picked up my family and the others from the Confederate ship *Etowah*. God was with us. Hannah and the children moved in blissful silence onto the deck. I dispatched two of my men in small rowboats to bring them to *The Planter*. Two black stewards on the *Etowah* had been enlisted in this conspiracy. Hannah, our two children, Hannah's thirteen-year-old daughter Clara Jones, and W. William Morrison, one of the black stewards on the *Etowah*, were quietly taken into the rowboat and boarded *The Planter*.

As they boarded, I could hear Hannah's voice quietly singing one of our favorite songs.

> *Wade in the water, wade in the water, children,*
> *Wade in the water, God's gonna trouble the waters.*

She held on to the power of music, and the music steadied us. She whispered to me that she'd tried so hard to calm them, but they were very anxious. She then insisted that each one of them pray silently.

All sixteen of us on board were bound together by faith, fear and a determination to be free. The women and children were sent to the bottom of the ship. Each man took his pre-assigned post. I prayed that we were also leaving bondage behind us. "Oh Lord, be with us on this fateful journey." I told them to all stay down in the hold, no matter what.

We had to keep up a steady, normal pace to give the impression that we were going about normal business. We came close to Fort Johnson, built in 1708 and repaired several times since. The Confederate forces occupied it in 1860, days after the Union's move to Fort Sumter initiated the siege. A crew member mentioned that the Union used it for storage. The Confederates enlarged it and it now had two batteries. They say that the first shots of the Civil War on Fort Sumter were fired from the east mortar battery in Fort Johnson. The date was April 12, 1861. The time was 4:30 a.m.

We passed it without triggering any suspicion, and continued east toward Fort Sumter and the main ship channel. The crew was nervous, and when we passed a guard boat patrolling the harbor that took no notice of us, we breathed a sigh of relief.

I rang for more steam, and realized I was holding my breath. "Full head! Full head of steam," I shouted.

John was in the engine-room, but unable to tell a crewman exactly where we were. "I gave it up to Captain Robert," he mumbled. "Gourdine and I were so weak we could hardly stand, and I saw his face was the color of ashes. We were frightened, and later found out that the others running the ship were too. Only Smalls seemed so be okay, and thank God he was our captain."

We passed a few more boats as we steamed toward Fort Sumter. I remained calm and saluted the gunboat with a whistle. Passing the next ones, I played my role as Captain Relyea and casually shouted out a greeting to the pilots.

About 4:15 a.m., we approached Fort Sumter. I saw her massive walls towering about fifty feet above the water. Since 1861, Confederate forces had occupied it and heavily fortified the fort. The channel was the only way ships could enter or leave the harbor. The Confederates had built a floating log boom across the channel, leaving a narrow gap near Fort Sumter to let blockade runners pass. In order to do this, they had to get close to Sumter's powerful cannons.

My crew knew this and was terrified. They also knew the other possible threat was that a ship might stop us and ask us to run an errand, which sometimes happened. We didn't tell the women and children about these alarming possibilities. Hopefully, they were sleeping down below. I had no way of knowing because Hannah asked me not to disturb them.

Hearing my crew's growing concerns, I assured them all would be fine. I noticed that Gourdine's knees were giving away, and then I heard the muffled sobbing of the women below. I asked my crew to pray without ceasing. We all knew we were now in "no-man's land"—halfway between slavery and freedom.

I steered *The Planter* directly beneath the walls of Fort Sumter. I kept to the shadows inside the pilothouse, hiding my face under the brim of the captain's hat. I deliberately pulled the whistle cord to give the appropriate signal: three shrill sounds and one hissing sound. That was the Confederate signal to pass. The sentinel called for the corporal guard, who commanded the guard-boat, to leave. The soldier at the fort didn't realize the boat was out of commission. After a long pause, the countersign came back: *Pass on by!* Here was another positive sign of God's plan of allowing us to pass.

I heard the sentry yell out as we passed, "Blow the damned Yankees to hell, or bring one of them in." I responded "Aye, aye Sir." Now I had to impersonate Captain Relyea. I leaned on the windowsill in the pilothouse and crossed my arms over my chest, just as Relyea did. My figure was trim like his, and I bore an unusual resemblance to him. In this dim light, no one could see that my complexion was a little darker than his.

We cleared Fort Sumter and continued on through the main ship channel. Gourdine told me what he and John had gone through in the engine room. "For at least a half hour, John and I expected to hear the boom of a big gun. When we were out of range, we fell to our knees and cried, prayed and sang Hallelujah songs."

When *The Planter* didn't turn east toward Morris Island, the Confederate guards at Fort Sumter must have realized our ship was headed toward the Union vessels stationed off Charleston Bar, a group of submerged sandbars that formed the outer limit of Charleston Harbor. They tried to signal the troops on Morris Island, but by the time they did, the steamer was too far away to be stopped.

At this moment, I pointed the ship toward the Union fleet, knowing it was the final part of our journey. We gave thanks to God for getting us through safely. I looked at my crew and raised my arms. "Succeed or die!"

Now we would face the armed Union warships. We had to let the Union know we were friendly, before they mistook our ship for an enemy warship.

With our paddle wheels churning through the dark water, the steamer headed toward the closest Union ship.

"Take down the flag!" I shouted, at the same time I hoisted the white bedsheet that Hannah brought with her to signal surrender. My hands shook like palm fronds in a storm.

I called down below. "Come on up! Unlock the hold! We've made it!"

They crept up the steps to glance around the deck, and then warily stepped up to it. After a long silent minute, I heard an outburst of tears, shouts and celebration. They sensed they could now make noise, as we were nearing the end of the journey. The children jumped up and down, hugging each other and the adults.

Our tears sprang from joy and gratitude; we had not been fired on or caught. For several joyful moments, we hugged and kissed—families and friends—and even danced in the small space available. We also gave thanks to God for getting us through safely. "Stay with us mighty Lord," Hannah began, "and help us reach our ultimate freedom."

I closed my eyes and held Hannah tightly against me. She clasped Elizabeth's hand and strapped Robert Jr.'s body to hers. "Help us, God. We're almost there. Please get us to our destination, just as You did with the Hebrews so long ago. Thank you, and Amen."

Heavy fog rolled in, hiding the steamer and the flag above. Would they see it before they began firing on us? Or, would they assume this Confederate ironclad ship would ram and sink them? Hannah never stopped praying or singing as we approached the ship.

What I didn't know then was that just as we passed Fort Sumter, Captain Relyea appeared at the wharf in Charleston and discovered his steamer was missing. He must have known what was going on, but chose not to sound an alarm right away. Had he done so, the Confederate soldiers at Sumter more than likely would have fired on *The Planter*.

The ship we approached was a 174-foot three-masted clipper ship, named the *Onward*. Because of this fog, we realized the ship's Captain could take no chances. He knew they could not out-run us.

Their Captain ordered his men to the battle stations. "All hands to quarters!" could be heard by everyone on both ships. Then he commanded his crew to turn the clipper so her port cannons were aimed at *The Planter*. I felt a chill run through me when they rotated their cannons toward us.

The fog lifted fleetingly, and at that moment their Captain saw the white flag of surrender.

"STAND DOWN!" he shouted. The gun crews were just seconds from unleashing an assault. Hannah looked up at me in amazement. "You did it, Cap! Your plan has succeeded."

There were no shots and no cannon fire. I heard shouts of *Hallelujah* and the clapping of hands from behind me on my ship. I looked into Hannah's eyes, filling with tears. We still didn't know what the Union soldiers would do. Would they even believe a slave crew? How would our story end?

The Captain pulled closer to us. His crew leaned against the rail as the Captain shouted, "Name of the steamer and what is your intent?"

After we answered, he ordered us to come alongside.

"Captain, Sir, what is your name?" I called out to him.

"I'm Captain Nickels," he answered, giving me a slight smile as he nodded his head.

I tipped my hat in greeting. My first words to Captain Nickels were, "Good morning, Sir! My name is Captain

Robert Smalls. I understand that this vessel may be of service to Uncle Abe. I've brought you some of the old United States guns, Sir! They were intended for Fort Sumter, Sir!"

There was a long pause. "Captain Smalls, tell me how you got possession of this vessel."

"Yes, Sir. I've piloted her for several years. She became a Confederate ship last year, and when I knew the officers were planning to take leave last night, this crew and I liberated her early this morning."

He looked at me for several long moments. "I must assume you knew that if you got caught, you'd have been shot, right?"

I nodded and gave him a nervous grin. "Yes, Sir, we all knew that. We took the chance for the promise of freedom."

He shook his head and slowly smiled. "Well, son, it looks like you've achieved it. You and these folks are free men and women! I congratulate you and the others for your courage."

Captain Nickels then sent six of his men to search *The Planter*. After a thorough examination down below, they returned to the deck. I asked their captain for a United States flag to display. He dispatched a crewman to bring me one.

"This ship is clean, and full of guns and explosives. If we'd taken a shot, she'd now be splinters and shards and you'd be blown to bits."

Every crewman on the *Onward* seemed to be in a state of disbelief, saying again and again, "We've never seen anything like this."

I turned to Hannah. "We didn't do this, Sugar; God did," I whispered quietly. She took my hand in hers.

"And you were His hands and feet to all of us onboard. Thank you, my dear husband, for this gift of freedom."

TEN

Hannah

We were an exhausted, dirty, hungry group of sixteen when we boarded the *Onward*. After the Captain and crew introduced themselves, Captain Nickels began discussions with Robert and our crew as to what should be done with us.

The questions and answers came from everyone. Even the children participated. "Where were you going? Weren't you afraid? What will you do now that you're free? Who planned this journey?"

We answered them as best we could with the information we had. Our crew gave all the credit to Robert. Captain Nickels asked Robert and me, "Where would you like to go?"

Robert stood tall, his arm wrapped around my shoulders. I smiled at Captain Nickels and told him that we didn't know what was ahead or where we would go. Robert added, "I believe we'd like to return to Beaufort, because my mother is there and I believe it would be a good place to start over."

After Captain Nickels' short conversation with Robert, he addressed the two of us. "I imagine there will be a considerable bounty on your head, Captain Smalls. You've just humiliated the Confederates in the Carolinas by your courageous act, and retribution will most likely be swift and violent."

Robert nodded slowly, giving the captain time to elaborate. "But that's for later consideration. Every one of you has had quite a day and a long night! My crew is setting up quarters for you to sleep, and they've prepared a quick meal as well." He stood up and stretched, looking nearly as tired as we were.

"Let me show you where you can find food. Tomorrow, we'll decide where to take you." (Several days later, Robert told me that May 12 and 13 were the longest days of his life).

After wishing us a good night's sleep, the Captain added, "Bear in mind that now you are free! You triumphed and brought yourselves and fourteen others to freedom. Congratulations!"

Those words were probably the most gratifying ones we would ever hear.

***

Captain Nickels ordered *The Planter* and its passengers to be taken sixty miles away to Port Royal and turned over to Admiral Samuel F. Du Pont, the commanding officer there. We took another ship, the *USS Augusta*, whose senior officer, Cdr. Enoch Parrot, arranged our transport. We were made comfortable and well-fed during that trip. At 10:00 p.m., we finally arrived at Port Royal.

The next day, Robert was called into Admiral Du Pont's office. "Captain Smalls, I congratulate you and salute you. You are a hero!" He grinned widely and offered his hand.

The Admiral promised to take care of us and told Robert he would continue employing him as a pilot onboard *The Planter*, due to his personal knowledge of the local waters. He also asked Robert if he were interested in piloting some of his other vessels, including his flagship, *Wabash*.

"That would be my honor, Sir! It would be a privilege," Robert responded eagerly.

He wanted Robert to join the Union Navy because of his knowledge of the inland waters, and that military branch was open to blacks. But the Navy had an educational requirement that my husband could not pass. Pilots had to be able to complete the curriculum in naval-training school, and to do that, they had to know how to read and write.

"I am so sorry, Admiral. In the South, it has been a law that slaves cannot be educated."

The Admiral's lips tightened. "Yes, I know, and I am very sorry about that. You are a very intelligent man."

"But I will do everything possible to learn to read at the first opportunity," Robert added, shaking his head with conviction. "And now that we're free, I promise you that Hannah and our children will be educated as well."

Admiral Du Pont was so impressed with Robert that he sent a dispatch to the Secretary of the Navy the following day. We were later shown this dispatch.

> *This man, Robert Smalls, is superior to any who has yet come into the lines; intelligent as many of them have been. His information has been most interesting, and portions of it of the utmost importance. I shall continue to employ Robert as a pilot on board The Planter for inland waters.*

Admiral Du Pont quickly organized an act of collaboration between the military services, and Robert was inducted into the U.S. Army, where they had no literacy requirements. His rank was lieutenant and his assignment was to Company B in the Thirty-third Regiment of the U.S. Colored troops. The Army then detailed him to the Navy, for whatever duties the Navy might require.

My husband's bravery became a national sensation as media coverage praised the "plucky Africans" for delivering into Union hands the first trophy from Fort Sumter. Equally valuable to the Union was the information on mine placements, rebel troop dispositions and a code book of Confederate flag signals, which Robert was able to provide to Admiral Du Pont.

The Planter and the cargo were appraised at $60,000, but the propaganda value of Robert's defection was priceless to the government, now struggling in the wake of many Confederate victories and mounting casualty reports. A grateful Congress awarded Robert and his crew a percentage of the value of the prize. Eventually, they gave him full command of *The Planter*. Robert continued to pilot *The Planter* for some time. He brought that ship and others into combat seventeen times in the remaining campaigns along the Carolina coast.

The reactions of the southern press to Robert's bravery were immediate and vengeful. The Confederate authorities paid an unintentional tribute to Robert's achievement, by offering a reward of $4,000 for his capture and return. Some of the rage was directed against the white officers who had abandoned *The Planter* on the night of May 12. Military messages reached General Robert E. Lee, who ordered the officers of *The Planter* to be punished appropriately. A military trial was held for Relyea, Hancock and Pitcher. All were found guilty of "disobedience of orders" and "neglect of duty." On appeal, the verdicts were set aside by a higher military court.

Robert and I were thrilled when we realized the northern public sentiment was expressed much more optimistically. An article in the May 20, 1862, issue of *New York Tribune* stated:

The country should feel doubly humbled if there is not magnanimity enough to acknowledge a gallant action, because it was the head of a black man that conceived it, and the hand of a black man who executed it. It would indeed become us to remember that no small share of the naval glory of the war belongs to the race which we have forbidden to fight for us; that one Negro has recaptured a vessel from a Southern privateer, and has brought away, from under the very guns of the enemy, where no fleet of ours has yet dared to venture, a prize whose possession a Commodore thinks worthy to be announced in a special dispatch.

That same newspaper issue carried the news that the U.S. House had passed a Senate bill and sent it forthwith for President Lincoln's signature. Enacted on May 30, 1862, the statute stipulated that the value of *The Planter* and its cargo "be appraised by a board of competent officers" and that one half of its value be divided equitably among "Robert Smalls and his associates, who assisted in rescuing her from the enemies of the government."

To us, the Negro community, this demonstrated how grateful the Union was for Robert's actions. It gave a large morale boost to the North, and provided Robert this well-deserved respect. And to further pay homage to him and his crew, on July 15, 1862, Admiral Du Pont sent the two flags carried by *The Planter* during its capture—The Confederate flag and the South Carolina state flag—to the Secretary of the Navy for historic preservation.

The Planter was appraised at over $9,000. Half that amount was awarded to the crew. (It was later learned that the real value of the ship at that time was $70,000). In August, Admiral Du Pont distributed the money, giving my husband Robert $1,500 and the rest of the crew

$400 each. Everyone was happy with this economic award. In the years to come, Robert spent more time and energy trying to get Congress to recognize the real value of *The Planter*. During those periods I reminded him that his motivation for capturing the ship had never been money; rather, it was about freedom, derived from the values his mother taught him as a young boy.

⁂

"Mama, when will we see Gramma Lydia?" asked Lizzie impatiently. We were traveling toward Beaufort and she was tired from the trip.

"Very soon, my sweet," I answered. Robert lifted her on his lap and told her a story.

"Lizzie and Robbie, look at the beautiful horses drinking from the river," I pointed out, as we passed this tranquil scene. The children loved animals, and this entertained them for a few moments.

Nearing the outskirts of Beaufort, I was stunned to see the changes in this town where Robert and I had married not that long ago. The once quiet streets were now crowded with Union soldiers, Negros from surrounding areas, and missionaries from the north. We could see the town was overflowing with people searching for food and shelter.

Happily, our homecoming with Lydia was full of laughter and affection. She joyfully embraced each one of us, enfolding us closely. That afternoon, she found rooms where we could all stay together until Robert found us a little house.

During the Union invasion, Lydia worked and lived in one of the churches that had been converted into a hospital, so she knew many people. She was recruited as a cook and paid $2.00 weekly, but she also prepared food for the officers and medics, as well as for the troops recovering in the hospital. She was popular with the Union officers in charge, who insisted she be paid as a domestic worker, and raised her salary to $10.00 a month.

"Little Elizabeth, you are so much bigger than I thought," Lydia said, enfolding both her grandchildren together.

"Gramma, you can call me Lizzie, like my family does. We are family too, aren't we? And I really like that name." Lizzie was clearly delighted with her Gramma.

Lydia laughed and replied, "Come here, Sugar, and enjoy your time with me. Let's get to know each other all over again, and I'll tell you some stories about our very special family."

By the time we arrived, the Union had been occupying the town for six months. They set up camps to help care for former slaves. And our family would receive adequate food, shelter, clothing and medical attention, as part of the government's effort to help the thousands of people whose former owners had fled months earlier.

It was an exciting, but uncertain, time for us. In several days, Robert would have to leave us here, since Admiral Du Pont had given him a position as a civilian pilot. We were pleased and grateful because he would earn three times as much as a Union private made. As a former slave, he never would have been allowed to serve in such a high position without Admiral Du Pont's intervention.

Before Robert left, and during our good-byes, I rested my palm gently on his chest.

"I've always called you Cap, and finally, now you are a Captain. But Wheelman or Captain or Pilot, you are my man—the father of our children. And I am very proud of you." We walked toward the water, linking our arms together. The sounds of the night enveloped us, and we felt a sense of peace when we looked up at the sky. "Look Baby, the sky has become an apricot afterglow," I pointed out.

"Dearest, there's nothing as lovely as a low country sunset, unless it's you," he whispered. I will miss this and my little family, but I'll return as soon as I can." We both smiled suddenly as we heard a barn owl hooting in the distance, and another one returning its call.

He kissed me softly. "That's us, every day we are away from each other."

ELEVEN

Robert

It was August of 1862 when I first met General David Hunter. He told me that he believed it was a military necessity to enlist blacks into the Union forces, because he doubted that the United States could win the war without them.

"It is imperative that we include the blacks in our military, Captain Smalls. President Lincoln has little chance of re-nomination and zero chance of re-election in November, unless the Union forces can turn the tide against the Confederacy. So I've had this great idea to send you and Reverend Mansfield French to Washington, D.C."

"Yes, Sir," I responded cautiously. "Why do you think we can help you?"

"I believe that together you could persuade the president and War Secretary Stanton to permit the enlistment of Port Royal "contrabands" into the Union Army." He smiled broadly. "This is a very delicate mission, yet one I am certain that you and French can handle beautifully."

Before I had an opportunity to discuss this assignment, he handed me a piece of paper. "This is my written statement for Secretary Stanton, requesting authorization for me to enlist black troops. When you see him, please elaborate from your personal experiences."

I was only twenty-four years old and just three months out of slavery. I had no formal education, yet I felt calm and reassured that this man had my interests at heart, as well as the country's. This meeting with General Hunter was the beginning of our long-lasting friendship that continued after the war and until his death.

Less than a week later, General Hunter greeted Rev. French and me warmly and seemed very enthusiastic about what he was about to propose.

"Gentlemen, how would you like to meet the president of the United States?"

Rev. French grinned and said, "Of course! What a great idea." I nodded in silent response.

"Because everyone is impressed and discussing the heroic act of Robert, the timing couldn't be better. Together you could convince President Lincoln that the time has come to re-assess his and the government's position. It is now time to allow the blacks to enlist in the military."

I believe my mouth fell open. Suddenly I found my voice. "Sir, I would personally recruit ten thousand black men who would be better soldiers than the present ones, because they will be fighting for their freedom!"

"I'm happy you agree," he added. "Because the presence of Robert Smalls in Washington is what will make this happen," he grinned. I could see that his eyes danced with excitement.

Plans were quickly put together for Rev. French and me to meet President Lincoln. Before sailing with him from Hilton Head to Washington D.C., we realized that we hadn't seen each other for any length of time since Hannah's and my wedding in 1856. And now, here we were, on August 16, 1862, waiting to be called into President Lincoln's office.

Both of us felt nervous as we waited in a dark-paneled room that reeked of tobacco and leather. Every wall was lined with books, and I commented that I'd never seen so many in one place.

"Books are our friends, Robert. It's very hard to part with them."

"I still don't read well enough to collect them, Rev. French. But I'm learning slowly and taking every opportunity to improve my skills."

Just then, a tall lanky gentleman came through the door and addressed us. "President Lincoln will see you now. Please remain standing until he sits, and if he stands up again, do the same." With an encouraging nod, he led us into the president's office.

President Lincoln stood, and I marveled at his height. He made me feel very small indeed. Smiling warmly, he approached us and extended his large hand.

"Captain Smalls, it is my great pleasure to meet you!" Shaking my smaller hand vigorously, he continued. "You are a hero, you know. I read your name in all the papers."

"Mr. President, it is an honor to meet you, Sir. Thank you so much for your kind words." I hoped my nervousness wasn't apparent.

The president turned to Rev. French and shook hands with him. "Reverend, it is wonderful to see you again." He gestured for us to be seated.

President Lincoln had met Reverend French on an earlier occasion when Frederick Douglass was present. Reverend French was one of a number of religious leaders attending that meeting.

"Mr. President, I have brought you a missive from General Hunter." I quickly handed him the written dispatch from the general to Secretary Stanton.

"Robert, I've heard many tales about your capture of that boat, but please tell me in your own words," he said, with a kind expression.

I began at the beginning, telling him how my crew had noticed and remarked about my resemblance to Captain Relyea. Once that idea took hold, I had developed an escape plan.

"Stop, please. I want Stanton in here to hear this!"

It took less than a minute for Mr. Edwin Stanton to enter the room. He was very imposing, with a wild gray beard and a firm midsection.

After being introduced to us, Mr. Stanton held our hands in his. Then he slapped Rev. French on the back.

President Lincoln was animated and smiling widely. "Ed, you'll love this. Smalls here sailed that boat right under the noses of the Rebels!"

Mr. Stanton leaned forward and asked me to tell him everything. So I did. I started out with my boyhood in Beaufort, and how I loved the water. I told them that later on I worked the docks in Charleston. And finally, how I became a wheelman on *The Plantor*.

"What a story you have, son. Continue, please," insisted President Lincoln.

I spoke about my family and how we dreamed of being free. I explained how I memorized the distinct signals for passing the forts, and how we prayed for a cloudy night and an outgoing tide. They listened attentively and asked intelligent questions.

"Captain, what would you have done if… well, what was your alternate plan?" Mr. Stanton asked me.

"Sir, we all agreed that if we were captured, we would hold each other's hands and jump into the sea."

There was a long moment of silence. Finally, the President asked, "With your women and children?"

I nodded slowly and met his gaze directly. "With all due respect, Mr. President, to live as a slave is not to really live. We wanted an equal chance in life. A chance to make our own choices, mistakes, and decisions."

Silence crept into the room. Eventually, President Lincoln cleared his throat and addressed me. "Robert, you now have that opportunity. What will you do?"

"Mr. President, Sir, I truly believe that the best way to predict the future is to create it."

President Lincoln chuckled and nodded. "I believe you are right about that, Mr. Smalls. I'd like you and Mr. Stanton to come up with some ideas about how to create a future for you and your people."

Then he turned to Mr. Stanton and Rev. French. "Now I understand why you both insist that we let the colored men fight with us. I've been urged to do this by Frederick Douglass and several others, who I greatly respect." He then handed Mr. Stanton the written missive I brought from General Hunter.

"Please arrange to have five thousand colored men from South Carolina recruited as soon as you can," he told Mr. Stanton.

I grinned broadly and thanked him. Turning to Rev. French, President Lincoln said, "You're a Methodist and I know you care about the colored people. Please see to it that those in occupied South Carolina have a chance at education. Not compulsory, but an opportunity."

My eyes teared up. Finally! Soon we'd see the day that all of us could learn to read and write.

Placing my hand over my heart, I spoke softly to the president. "Mr. President, Sir, thank you very much. I am speechless."

President Lincoln took my hands in his. "I hope not," he grinned.

When we walked back to the ante-room, I felt like I'd just said goodbye to a good friend.

On our return to Beaufort, I personally delivered an order from the president and the secretary of war to General Rufus Saxton. This order, dated August 25, 1862, authorized the enlistment of five thousand African American troops. This was the first unit of black troops officially admitted by President Lincoln into the Union Army. I also volunteered for duty with this regiment, but was told I was needed in the Navy.

General Saxton, Secretary Stanton and President Lincoln were pleased with the order to enlist black troops. Eventually, 285,000 blacks were recruited into the U.S. Army. Later I learned that these men's efforts provided the margin of victory for the Union. That gave me great assurance that my efforts had been worthwhile.

TWELVE
Elizabeth

True to his word, Daddy returned to Beaufort and continued the educational campaign for former black slaves that he helped develop during his time in Washington D.C. Daddy's earnings as a pilot and as a storekeeper (he opened a small store right after he returned), gave him the means to secure private housing for our little family, including Gramma Lydia.

He started by raising money to support the education and development for new working opportunities for the formerly enslaved people. This plan was entitled the *Port Royal Experiment* and was written in Washington, D.C. After he put this plan together, Daddy was sent to pilot *The Planter* to Philadelphia, and he decided to take our family with him. During those seven weeks away from Port Royal, he was able to raise a lot of money for the *Port Royal Experiment* by giving speeches and sharing his story.

We then went to New York, where Reverend French's and Daddy's fund-raising efforts continued. They spoke to large audiences who were eager to listen and learn.

During those times, Mama and Daddy often discussed things quietly, and I eavesdropped when I could. I heard that some people were hostile toward them, but it didn't seem to affect them and their audiences. Rev. French generally spoke about the *Port Royal Experiment*, and Daddy talked about our escape on *The Planter*. Mama told us that Daddy's natural talent for storytelling fascinated the spectators.

A very exciting event took place while we were fundraising in New York. President Lincoln issued his *Preliminary Emancipation Proclamation*, which was to go into effect on January 1, if the Confederate states had not ended their rebellion.

"Oh Baby, this is so much like our personal journey to freedom!" exclaimed Mama, snuggling against his chest.

Daddy turned to me and a slow smile spread across his face. "How well do you remember that journey, Lizzie? Do you remember many details or conversations?

"Of course I do, Daddy. I remember it all," I said petulantly. "I wasn't a baby, you know."

Mama smiled and reflected. "Just think about all the opportunities we've been given since that day."

"After this proclamation, there is no doubt that the formerly enslaved people will be legally free in January, when it goes into effect." Daddy was beaming.

We went back to Philadelphia, where we were warmly welcomed in many places. Daddy spoke at the National Hall on Market Street. The city's district attorney introduced him to several prominent citizens. One of them exclaimed, "I would rather vote for this man, Smalls, for president, than for any Democrat in the land."

Reverend French returned to Port Royal, and we went back to New York. When Daddy spoke at Shiloh Presbyterian Church, many African Americans crowded into the venue, and he was received with deafening cheers. They also gave him a large gold medal. One side showed the Charleston Harbor with an image of *The Planter* headed toward Fort Sumter and the Union fleet. The other side of the medal was inscribed with: "*Presented to Robert Smalls* *by the colored people of NY, Oct. 2nd, 1862, as a token of their regard for his heroism, his love of liberty, and his patriotism."*

Mama and Daddy were very touched by that gift, coming from the hearts of the people. They talked about it often, commenting that they understood that racism in some people in the North was equal to the Southerners. They realized that hatred brought about violence. The next day we learned that one man was assaulted near the church, and that a planned riot had been foiled, because the protesters had begun their attack before the meeting adjourned.

Among the Sea Island blacks, Daddy was all but worshipped. He was cheered with great ceremony by those who never tired of hearing him talk about his gallant service and dangerous escape. To many, he was their hero and idol—the man who had helped them reach freedom.

We also heard that many in the South were unhappy with Daddy's growing fame. In fact, when the Confederate newspapers were notified about his speaking tours and their positive reception, they were furious with the North for glorifying him. And when we returned to Port Royal, we were warned that he was still a "wanted man."

Daddy refused to be intimidated, and returned to his duties as a pilot for the Union. An outbreak of yellow fever began a week before our return, debilitating the soldiers and taking its toll. They took precautions, but many weakened, and some died from the bites of infected mosquitoes. Maj. Gen. Ormsby Mitchel replaced Hunter as Commander of the Department of the South in early September of 1862, and moved his staff from Hilton Head to Beaufort. After only five days, he succumbed to the disease.

My father saw his friend Admiral Du Pont in Beaufort, along with Capt. John Rodgers. Both had come to be pallbearers at Mitchel's funeral.

Daddy was surprised by the condescending tone of a question Capt. Rogers asked him. "Captain Smalls, has your head been turned by the attention you received on these long money- making visits?"

Daddy answered him calmly, with a genuine smile. "My head was turned one way the entire time I was in the North—toward Port Royal."

I knew my father was sincere in his efforts to help the Union in any way he could. A few years later, when he repeated that story, he made a confession. "As a free man, we, as a family, could have easily stayed in the North instead of returning to the South, where a heavy bounty hung over my head and threatened my life. But I knew we were meant to fight the battle here."

Shortly after our return to Beaufort, Daddy was told that *The Planter* was no longer under naval jurisdiction. Admiral Du Pont had turned it over to the Army's Quartermaster Corps. He was informed that Daddy would now be piloting other vessels for the Navy.

The little store Daddy had opened was beneficial to the Freedmen, who now earned money as part of the *Port Royal Experiment*. They needed supplies, and his store provided those. He didn't realize that he'd soon be making a large weekly profit. And to enhance his delight, the continued success of the *Port Royal Experiment* allowed General Saxton to create a new regiment of black soldiers—the First South Carolina Volunteer Infantry Regiment. This squadron incorporated the men from Hunter's regiment, who were furloughed, as well as his own soldiers. He brought in some new recruits from Georgia,

Florida, and South Carolina as well. Now he had over six hundred soldiers.

General Saxton set aside a day in November as one of "thanksgiving and praise." The next year President Lincoln issued his *Thanksgiving Proclamation*, dedicating the last Thursday of November as a holiday. Beaufort celebrated Thanksgiving by singing the spiritual *Roll, Jordan Roll*, followed by a sermon and a long speech given by General Saxton, who encouraged young black men to enlist in the service.

My father told General Saxton that, instead of continuing with his very successful little store, he was convicted that he should enlist as a private in Saxton's new regiment.

General Saxton asked him, "Why, Captain, if you are making fifty dollars a week?"

Daddy answered, "How can I expect to keep my freedom unless I fight for it? What if we have to fight again for our freedom? What good would my fifty dollars do then? Indeed Sir, I would enlist even if I were making a thousand dollars a week."

General Saxton repeated this exchange to encourage the young black men to enlist. He knew that my father was a hero to many throughout the country; especially to the African Americans in Port Royal. Miss Charlotte Forten, the first African American teacher from the North to teach in the South, heard Daddy's speech that day. She was motivated by it, and as fate would have it, she soon became my teacher at the Penn School.

This South Carolina regiment saw action and proved their courage and skill. Saxton wrote to Stanton: "It is admitted upon all hands that the Negroes fought with a coolness and bravery that would have done credit to veteran soldiers. There was no flinching, and no attempt at cruelty when successful. They were fighting to vindicate their manhood and they did it very well."

Even though my father wanted to enlist in the regiment, he finally decided against it. He never told us why, but Mama thinks perhaps Admiral Du Pont convinced him that his skills were urgently needed in the Navy.

THIRTEEN
Elizabeth

When I was six years old, Daddy enrolled me in the Penn School across the river on St. Helena Island. My first instructor was Charlotte Forten, who taught her classes in the Brick Church from October 1862 to March 1864. Miss Forten had volunteered to come south when she learned about the educational mission my Daddy and others had initiated during his time spent in Washington, D.C.

I loved Miss Forten, who was a beautiful, cultured and very smart lady. She encouraged her students to be curious and courageous. She was the granddaughter of prominent black abolitionists, and had taught for several years in New England before coming to South Carolina.

Daddy asked me every evening what I learned that day.

"Lizzie, tell me the hardest subject you studied today." He began. "And then what you learned about it."

"Oh Daddy, Miss Forten makes it all easy. She knows everything, and really wants us to learn too," I beamed. "She loves to hear my questions and answer them. Of course, I work hard to try to be the best student in the class."

My father's appreciation for education began with himself, extended to his wife and children, and then to the newly-freed black children in Beaufort. After that, he concentrated on all the black and white children of South Carolina, and then helped to frame and start up a program of higher education for the entire black community.

Daddy had finally realized his long-time dream: he learned to read and write! He hired a private tutor, Miss Rosa Colley, another teacher at the Penn School. When he was here in Beaufort, he would awaken at 5:00 a.m. to study the lessons she left him the previous day. In the afternoons, Miss Colley came to our house to spend another hour working with him.

When he was away piloting for the government, he tried to set aside some time to study every day. After about nine months, he could read Frederick Douglass's papers himself. We celebrated his accomplishment.

"Oh Daddy, I know how much this means to you," I applauded him. "I'm so happy we learned to read and write at the same time! You've worked very hard for this moment!" He beamed, his deep brown eyes shining, and gathered me in his arms. I used my finger to wipe away a tear escaping from the corners of his eyes.

We enjoyed the special evenings when he read news articles about our country. One night he brought us a speech that Frederick Douglass had delivered in 1852, entitled *What Is the Fourth of July to the Slave?* The speech was presented in Rochester, New York, to a local antislavery women's group on July 5, 1852. One of his crewmen had a copy and gave it to Daddy to share with us.

After reading most of it, my father asked for our opinions. Then he gave us his.

"Many historians and I consider this effort to be Douglass' finest speech up to now. But of course, I haven't read all of his work," he chuckled. "I believe it's one of the most powerful American political speeches ever written."

Turning to Mama he announced, "Hannah, you'll be the next one to learn to read. And then your daughters, and anyone else in our family who doesn't already read." He was serious. Daddy considered it an honor to counsel so many blacks to actively seek an education.

Our country entered its third year of war on January 1, 1863. We were weary of bloody battles, but that day turned out to be a blessing to so many of us. President Lincoln issued the long-awaited *Emancipation Proclamation* on New Year's Day—the day many had dreamed of for years.

Celebrations exploded in the Union-occupied South, as well as throughout the North. In Boston, three thousand black and white abolitionists, including Frederick Douglass and William Lloyd Garrison, honored the day at Tremont Temple. Four thousand African Americans marched through the streets of Norfolk, Virginia, beating drums and singing, while carrying American flags.

The proclamation officially freed many people in parts of the South controlled by the Union, including those at Port Royal. General Saxton ordered a celebration on Port Royal Island. Daddy was away on a ship, but the rest of us attended the celebration at the First South Carolina Volunteer Infantry's headquarters that morning. The band played joyfully and the stage was filled with dignitaries. Following the reading of the *Emancipation Proclamation* and a prayer, Rev. Mansfield French presented the colors to Col. T.W. Higginson, the regiment's white leader. The silk flag was a gift from the New York Church of the Puritans and embroidered with "The Year of Jubilee has come!"

Suddenly we heard an elderly voice break into song! "My Country, 'Tis of Thee" filled the air and was quickly accompanied by several female voices. Soon, everyone was energized. Higginson eventually broke in and asked that *only* the newly-freed African American men and women sing the patriotic words. He felt their voices should fill the air. No one in attendance would ever forget that jubilant tribute paid to the blacks on that day of Jubilee.

Mama and Gramma Liddy were crying, along with many others. One lady turned to us and said, "This is the first day we've ever had a country. And this is the first flag we've had that promised anything to our people." I felt sad that Daddy wasn't there to share these precious moments with everyone.

———

I was the one to tell Mama that Robbie was not well. It was springtime, when the weather was perfect, but my little brother had developed a dry cough.

"Mama, come over here quickly!" I shouted. "Robbie just fell off the chair!"

Mama hurried to pick him up. Feeling his forehead, she said "Lizzie, he seems very warm, and he's been coughing a lot lately."

I nodded, since I often felt him burning up during our play time together.

She frowned, deep concern covering her face.

We found a doctor to examine him. "It looks like he has whooping cough. Has he been around an infected person?" the doctor asked.

Mama shook her head. "I don't think so, Doctor, but we do have visitors stop by from time to time."

The doctor took a deep breath. "Sometimes a contaminated object, something sneezed on or sucked on like sheets, can cause this bacterial infection." He told us to make a juice with a sliced turnip covered with brown sugar. "Give this to him every few hours, as well as lemon and honey tea." Mama listened quietly and nodded.

"There is an outbreak in Beaufort now. I've seen freedmen and even Union soldiers infected. I am so sorry. Try to keep him cool and give him plenty of fluids."

"Robbie, please get well," I begged him, rocking him in my arms. "You're the only baby brother I have." He smiled at the sound of my voice and reached out to touch my face. Between tears, I reassured him, "We all love you so much."

We couldn't believe how quickly he weakened, and my poor Mama was beside herself. Daddy kept assuring us he was healing, until one afternoon he just stopped breathing. Mama and I took turns holding him, sobbing as he wheezed and struggled for his final breaths.

None of us was prepared for this. My Gramma wasn't home when he died, but she collapsed when she returned and saw his body. Falling to her knees, she prayed loudly for his soul, and for the Lord to give us all strength. Mama was trying to hold us together, but she and Daddy had moments where they fell apart. I was only a child, but knew I needed to help them get through this grief. Little Robbie was only sixteen months old.

Even as a child, I was overcome with sorrow. I didn't know how to handle it, or where to turn, so I prayed to God. Both my parents, and even my Gramma Lydia, tried to console me. This was the first tragedy we'd suffered as a family. Mama crumbled with despair, and Daddy begged Rev. French to stay with us, even after the funeral. He helped me understand that life is fragile, but that Robbie was at peace, and with God now. Slowly, each of us somehow climbed our way back into life.

After the funeral, I returned to school and looked to Miss Forten for encouragement. My classmates were helpful too, and I gradually came to accept what death meant. In my head, I can still clearly see Robbie's beautiful face. I know I'll remember him every day, and that will keep him close in my heart.

FOURTEEN

Elizabeth and Robert

My parents had a lot on their minds in the fall of 1863. They told me Mama would have a baby around Christmastime, and that made me miss little Robbie. Still, I hoped that this new baby would bring back some happiness to our family.

Daddy was working with the Union at Port Royal, and they were struggling to capture Charleston. They had taken Battery Wagner on Morris Island, after a very long siege against the Confederates, but Charleston was still under Confederate control. Daddy told us that because the Union was desperate to get that city, it was consistently shelled, as were the fortifications in the harbor. Daddy said this bombardment lasted 576 days—the longest siege in American history.

My father didn't talk much about these difficult days, but he did share with us one incredible adventure, where he confronted both the enemy and his own superior officer, Captain Nickerson.

In late December, he returned to piloting *The Planter* and delivering supplies to the Union troops on Morris Island. Steering it through a narrow creek, *The Planter* was caught in a crossfire from the battery at Secessionville and a Union ship. Daddy says the Confederates recognized *The Planter* as their lost ship, and tried to recapture her.

The shelling was intense and *The Planter* was struck often. But since the shells came from such a high bluff, the ship was not hit below the waterline and didn't sink.

Captain Nickerson was in command and Daddy served as his pilot. When the captain realized that the intense shelling caused great damage to the ship, he ordered Daddy to beach *The Planter* and surrender.

"Captain, Sir, if we surrender you will be treated as an officer. But the rest of us are runaway slaves. The Confederates will show us no mercy." The captain again shouted out his order to beach the ship.

"Not by a damn sight will I beach *The Planter*," Daddy shouted in return. "I can and will steer the ship to safety."

Captain Nickerson panicked, and fled from his post to hide in the coal bunker. Daddy calmly took over the captain's seat, but first called Samuel Chisholm to take the wheel momentarily while he ran to the coal bunker and latched the door from the outside. Then he returned to steer the ship safely back to Morris Island.

"Oh Daddy, weren't you frightened?" I asked anxiously.

"Of course I was, my sweet child, but I didn't have time to think about that. I had to get her out of gun range, so I captained her to Morris Island and delivered the provisions and the crew safely."

He went on. "If we had abandoned her, you realize we would have been captured. I would have been executed in accordance with Confederate policy."

The ship was met by Major General Quincy A. Gillmore, the department commander. Daddy led him to the coal bunker and released Captain Nickerson. That same evening, Admiral Du Pont dismissed Captain Nickerson from the U.S. Navy for cowardice and desertion.

Daddy was rewarded nicely for his selfless act of bravery. The chief quartermaster of the Department of the South, J.J. Elwell, immediately issued an order to the chief assistant quartermaster on Folly and Morris Islands.

Sir: You will please place Robert Smalls in charge of the United States transport The Planter as captain. He brought her out of Charleston Harbor more than a year ago, running under the guns of Sumter, Moultrie, and the other defenses of that stronghold. He is an excellent pilot, of undoubted bravery, and in every respect worthy of that position. This is due him as proper recognition of his heroism and services. The present captain is a coward, though a white man. Dismiss him and give the steamer to this brave black man.

What a wonderful honor for my father! He had served on that steamer beginning as a deck-hand, then was promoted to wheelman under the Confederates, then from pilot to Captain under the Union. He became the first black Captain of an Army vessel! What a remarkable journey! Even the *New York Tribune's* correspondent wrote about Elwell's order: *For simple justice to a brave and loyal Negro, officially acknowledged, has seldom been equaled in this or any other department.*

That article was printed in newspapers across the country. But even as the Captain of *The Planter,* my father was still a civilian. Yet he was handsomely paid. His new position paid $150 per month—double his previous salary. His new salary was just a little less than what a Union major earned.

The salary increase was timely. My little sister, Sarah Voorhess Smalls, was born that same day: December 1, 1863. And she was born free! Mama and the rest of us rejoiced at her arrival, though sadly, Daddy wasn't home that day. He was rescuing *The Planter*.

―

In the spring of 1863, with the Union Army's new black troops in place, there was renewed enthusiasm to capture Charleston. Admiral Du Pont gathered his ships—now a nine-ship combat flotilla. *The Charleston Post and Courier* wrote: *In the spring of 1863, the most powerful naval squadron ever assembled under the Stars and Stripes gathered at Port Royal to attack the Confederate Citadel at Charleston.*

I, Robert Smalls, fought in that battle, having been asked to participate by Lieutenant Rhind, due to our experiences in previous combat missions. It is interesting that when I was addressing an assembly in New York, one of the questions asked to me was, "What about the $4,000 reward the Confederates have offered for your capture?" My response was, "The only way I would return to Charleston would be heading a Union fleet ordered to capture the city."

I did not lead that attack, but I was honored to be a part of it.

The flotilla passed Morris Island without drawing fire from the Confederates. They unleashed their guns at Cummings Point, at the narrow mouth of the Charleston harbor. The Union did not return fire, because our target was Fort Sumter.

When we were in range of the fort, between it and Fort Moultrie, both forces unleashed a barrage of gunfire. I saw one ironside veer off course, blocking the other ships behind it. It was difficult maneuvering the ships in the narrow channel, with fire coming from both directions.

I was in the *Keokuk* at the rear of the line of vessels, but I knew I could get us out safely.

I asked Lieutenant Rhind if I could proceed forward, and he consented. I immediately ordered my engineers to pick up speed and I steered my ship around the vessels lined up in front. It didn't take long to bring the *Keokuk* to within striking distance of Fort Sumter. Our gunners shelled Fort Sumter for over thirty minutes, taking heavy fire from the guns at the fort. We received ninety rounds of fire and nineteen of them struck below the water line, giving us a strong possibility of sinking.

The waves were extremely high, causing the ships to toss and turn. Unfortunately, my wheelman, sitting next to me, was hit in the face by cannon fire. His blood splattered all over me. I rushed to him to help out, but I could hardly see. In the end, my wheelman recovered, but was blinded by the fire. The barrage had also damaged my eyesight, but did not blind me.

The *Keokuk* started drifting aimlessly and lurching crazily, finally plunging underneath the waves. Working fast and furiously, in spite of my damaged eye, I struggled to bring her upright. We wrestled her for another hour, after which Lieutenant Rhind decided the *Keokuk* was no longer seaworthy and ordered me to withdraw the ship from the engagement.

I was disappointed, but piloted her to safety off Morris Island. Rhind and his crew came to help, and we worked through the night to plug up the holes in the *Keokuk*.

She was repaired by 7:30 a.m. Just as we started her up, another robust wind developed, triggering enormous waves. She sank upright, only minutes after the crew was rescued by another ship.

Five of the remaining ships were damaged that night, but the *Keokuk* received the worse damage. Never before had I seen a vessel under such fire. We were closer to the fort and nearer than any other ship, and we were overcome by this encounter. The Confederates on Morris Island beach watched the *Keokuk* go down, tossing their hats in celebration. I felt a profound sorrow.

Admiral Du Pont made the decision to leave the *Keokuk*, now filling up with sand, where she fell. To this day she still lies off Morris Island. The Confederates, under the cover of darkness, salvaged some of the equipment from the *Keokuk*, most notably the two massive Dahlgren guns. One of them remains as the only physical sign of this battle on April 7, 1863. It will always be a reminder of one of the most incredible salvage jobs of the Civil War.

My services with *The Planter* continued until the end of the war in April 1865. I met with her once again. In September of 1866, I was ordered to take her to Baltimore for decommissioning. That was another heartbreaking ending for me, since we'd worked together for several years.

FIFTEEN
Elizabeth

In 1863, Congress passed "An Act for Collection in the Insurgent District," which held southern landowners in areas under northern control responsible for property taxes. Hundreds of plantations and homes went on the auction block when these taxes were not paid. One of them was the house of Daddy's former masters in Beaufort. This was the big house at 511 Prince Street, where Daddy was born and he and his mother lived as slaves under the McKee family.

The last owner, William DeTreville, bought the house from Henry McKee after graduating from Princeton University. He returned to Beaufort and practiced law for a few years and then departed. The requirements for purchasing these houses were different for civilians than for soldiers. Soldiers had to put down only 25 percent of the accepted bid amount and were given three years to pay off the rest. Civilians, like my father, had to pay the full amount in cash. Daddy had the cash, thanks to his Congressional prize money.

On January 28, 1864, the house on Prince Street came up for auction. Robert Smalls put in the winning bid of $665. The house was appraised at $700. This purchase was a personal victory for my father.

He walked over to the Episcopal Church where Gramma Lydia was cooking, while Mama was scrubbing the discarded pews. She and others were converting the "hospital church" back to its former purpose.

"Hello Mama," he grinned, leaning down to rest his forehead against hers. "Come sit down a bit, Mama. Hannah and I got some news for you."

She sat down hesitantly, wiping her hands across her apron. "I hope it's good, but Lordy, you better tell me now."

Daddy and Mama grinned at each other. Each of them took one of Gramma Lydia's hands. "We just bought us a real pretty place that might feel just like home to you," he said softly. His brown eyes twinkled as she tried to follow this.

"Where is it, son?"

"It's on Prince Street," he teased. Mama's smile was huge.

Gramma Lydia's eyes widened and her hands flew to her mouth as his words sank in.

"We're going back to the house where you lived and worked, but this time, you'll live inside it, and not behind it!"

Mama said Gramma Lydia looked like she would faint. Instead, she told them about the warm happy feeling that floated through her body as tears of joy slipped down her cheeks.

Daddy told us often how happy he was to have been able to buy it. "I am proud of the fact that I am living in a dwelling built on the very ground where I was born. The old homestead and its surroundings are mine, and one day I will leave them for my children to enjoy."

Other former slaves were also able to purchase houses at auction, including our friend Morrison, the tinsmith who escaped with us on *The Planter*. Daddy was told that blacks bought seventy-five to eighty houses in Beaufort. Whites also bought up auctioned houses, and two of Henry McKee's other properties in town were among them. This all happened after the white owners had fled and the Union officers came to occupy the town.

Some years later, the former owner of the house sued Daddy to get the house back. DeTreville and his father, serving as his lawyers, took this lawsuit all the way to the Supreme Court in 1878. They lost the lawsuit, and Daddy prevailed. This litigation became the benchmark for many other families, who were also allowed to remain in their newly purchased houses.

Mama and Daddy, Gramma Lydia, Sarah and I moved into our new home. My sister and I learned the stories of their past from our father and Gramma Lydia: how he lived in the cabin behind the home from birth to twelve years of age, and then Lydia stayed there after he left Beaufort. He visited his mother in that home a few times after that. Now, at twenty-five, he owned the house and was the Captain of an army vessel.

The day of the purchase, Daddy and Mama went back to visit the house. Daddy surveyed his land and home. He quietly considered all of this for a long moment.

A slow smile spread across his face as he stood with Mama on the porch. He rubbed her back, feeling the warmth of her skin through the thin fabric of her dress.

"Sugar, we have just received another enormous blessing. You and I will sleep in the master bedroom. My mother will have her own room, the girls will eventually share another room. We even have space enough for family members to visit. But most importantly, you and I will come and go as we please. No more curfew for us ever!"

Mama's grin broadened. She nodded, and placing her finger under his chin, she leaned forward to meet his lips. "Captain, you have done it again," she murmured softly.

In early May of 1864, my father left us in Port Royal and set out on his second trip to Philadelphia. He was unhappy to leave us, but took comfort in knowing that his wife, mother and daughters would be safe in their new home. As Captain of *The Planter*, it was his responsibility to deliver her to the Navy Yard in Philadelphia for repairs and refurbishment after constant Confederate fire. He would remain there until the job was completed. It took over seven months to finish the work.

Daddy was proud to captain the ship that had changed his life and that of his family. Philadelphia was booming due to the war, and had constructed private shipyards to build navy vessels. Dozens of private companies manufactured swords, sabers, firearms and flags for the government. During the time Daddy was in Philadelphia, he reported to the assistant quartermaster's office. He noticed there was an underlying hostility toward the blacks, and experienced it firsthand. Yet he also received kindness and respect from many.

The initial estimate to repair the ship was $25,000 to $29,000. Ultimately, it cost more than $40,500. Interestingly, Daddy said the Navy was willing to spend so much more to restore this ship because the actual value exceeded the appraisal value used to determine the prize money given to him and the others onboard. At the time the prize money was given out, *The Planter's* value was assessed at $9,000.

A week after he arrived in Philadelphia, Beaufort voted for him, in absentia, to serve as a South Carolina delegate to the National Union Party's convention in Baltimore to choose a presidential nominee. The party had temporarily changed its name to "National Union," hoping to appeal to more Democrats. Twelve whites and four blacks were chosen as delegates. General Saxton was one of the whites and my father was among the blacks who were elected. Daddy couldn't attend the convention, yet this nomination attracted both attention and anger in the South. *The Charleston Mercury* reminded its readers that *"Smalls had carried a steamboat to the Yankees two years ago."*

As it turned out, the Convention Committee on Credentials would not seat any South Carolinians, black or white. Arguments were discussed as to why. Some said it was because they represented an occupied area instead of a state government. Other countered it was because they were an integrated delegation. Wendell Phillips, the respected abolitionist, wrote: *Every sane man knows that South Carolina was rejected because it sent black delegates. No evasion can rub that spot out of Baltimore garments, and it is of too much significance to be omitted or confused in an Anti-Slavery record.*

Abe Lincoln was nominated as the Union candidate for president. Andrew Johnson, a War Democrat, was named his running mate. Since Johnson was from Tennessee, Lincoln hoped his presence on the ticket would appeal to southerners. Hannibal Hamlin, the present vice-president, had no more political value.

In the meantime, Daddy wasted no time, and continued to speak wherever he was invited. My teacher, Charlotte Forten, had given Daddy letters of introduction to some of the leading abolitionists in the city. They welcomed him into their midst, and he never tired of speaking to large or small groups about his adventures.

He spoke to a group of Philadelphia's black citizens at Mother Bethel, which was the mother church of the African Methodist Episcopal (AME) denomination. We heard from others that he won the admiration of the audience.

He began humbly: "I am not a speaker, but always feel happy if I can say anything to strengthen the hearts of the noble men who are battling for freedom. It is for the cause of freedom that I am here before you this evening." An explosive applause rang out after those words, so he continued: "Although born a slave, I always felt that I was a man and ought to be free, and I would be free or die."

That statement followed him everywhere.

A week later, Daddy spoke for the *Colored People's Union League Association* and then at other gatherings during his stay in Philadelphia. A group called the *Fraternal Association* also invited him to make a presentation. They were established in 1861, "for the purpose of relieving the wants and distresses of each other in the time of affliction and death, and to establish and maintain a permanent and friendly intercourse among themselves in their social relations in life."

On June 21, the *Fraternal Association* invited my father to an elegant dinner. He was very impressed with the menu: terrapin, beef a la mode, boiled ham, lobster salad, and rice purlieu. There were various desserts, punch and cigars. This festive banquet was lauded in the *Christian Recorder* as: *one of the finest we have ever attended.* That evening Daddy met an important figure and new friend, with whom he would remain close during the rest of his life.

Octavius Catto was an influential African American leader in Philadelphia, and a highly regarded teacher in the city's *Institute for Colored Youth.* Born a free man in Charleston, Catto was mostly raised in the North. He returned to Charleston when his father was hired as the minister of Philadelphia's First African Presbyterian Church.

"Rev. Catto, what have you been doing here since that time?" my father asked in conversation.

"Well, my Daddy passed down to me his passionate concerns about emancipation, the right of blacks to vote and the importance of education. So you might say that I'm following in his footsteps," he smiled.

When my father learned that Catto taught math and English at the *Institute for Colored Youth*, he asked if he would be willing to work with him privately to improve his English. He hoped that through him he could meet Frederick Douglass, and fortunately, that took place shortly after this event. The two men bonded, and Daddy learned more about championing equal rights and advocating education for all. "Another friendship that was meant to happen," he told us.

As an energetic six-year-old, I was thrilled to discover that my parents were hosting a wedding in our new home. Lavinia Wilson, who was part of our little group on *The Planter* during our escape, had become a good friend of our family. She was also like another daughter to my parents. I was happy to be able to participate in the wedding. Gramma Lydia made me a pretty pink gown, and I was allowed to toss rose petals when Lavinia and her husband walked through the garden into the house for the ceremony.

This wedding was written up in the local newspaper. Mama saved the article and it mentioned that: *Captain Robert Smalls now owns the house of his former master, where he himself was born.* It went on to describe the rooms as *tastefully decorated and illuminated. A table was furnished bountifully and in a style creditable to any of the chivalry.*

This wedding included friends Daddy met after he seized *The Planter*. Reverend French married the couple and Brig. Gen. Saxton and his wife, Matilda, were guests, as well as some of his staff. Mama invited a few of the "first families of Freedmen,"—some of whom were relatives to the *very elite* of South Carolina. They were the formerly enslaved children of wealthy white planters and their female slaves. Once ignored by Beaufort society, they were now leading it.

Other elegant dinner parties followed, and I spent the next several years playing hostess and learning etiquette. Of course I was taught some of that at the Penn School by Miss Forten, yet I enjoyed participating in stylish events, which I later practiced in my own home. As soon as she could walk, my little sister Sarah followed me around, and basked in the attention we both received.

SIXTEEN

Hannah

My husband, Robert, and a white seaman on his ship, were walking to the shipyard from their quarters in Philadelphia. It began to rain just as they reached the shipyard, and the rain continued all day. When they left to return to their quarters, they were quickly drenched and decided to ride the streetcar. After finding two seats under cover, they sat down and watched the conductor as he approached them.

"Boys, move forward to the open platform so that these white passengers can be seated inside," he directed. He spoke without shame and did not ask them politely.

Robert rose, and looked the man in the eye. "Sir, I will concede my seat to the white men," he told him. "But please tell me why."

The conductor replied, "We allow no man of your skin color in the cars. You must go forward."

My husband had one more question for him. "Does the law require black men to ride on the platform?"

"Yes, it does."

"Then I will not disobey the law. I shall leave the car," he said, turning toward the door. "And you, Sir, will learn soon enough that all men are created equal, and should be treated that way."

Loyal to his Captain, the white pilot refused to remain in the car. He trailed Robert, his jaw tensing, and stopped momentarily to address the conductor. "I will proudly follow my Captain."

As they walked back into town, he said, "Captain Smalls, why didn't you tell him you are a national hero?"

My husband chuckled. "He will realize that in due time. Insults hurt, but they won't stop me from carrying out a campaign to eliminate racial segregation on streetcars and all types of public transportation."

Robert Smalls never mentioned the incident during his remaining six months in Philadelphia, and the country didn't hear about it until after he returned to Port Royal. On January 13, 1865, some of the city's leading citizens sponsored a protest meeting at Philadelphia's Concert Hall to deal with the nation's streetcar situation. In his speech, J. Miller McKim, a longtime antislavery advocate who brought some missionaries from Philadelphia to Port Royal, described how my father "had been forced off a streetcar because of his complexion."

Newspapers across the country jumped on the story. They were united in purpose: *Turning Smalls away was a disgrace to American civilization.* The upheaval prompted Pennsylvania state senator Morrow B. Lowry to sponsor a bill to end streetcar segregation. But it took two more years for streetcars to be desegregated. My husband's friend and tutor, Mr. Catto, fought hard to get this passed into law. Four years later, Catto was shot and killed by a white man during the first election in Philadelphia that permitted blacks to vote.

※

In the early fall of 1864, my husband fulfilled another dream. He learned that his good friend Rev. French was in Philadelphia. Rev. French invited him to meet late one afternoon for some food and drink.

After the pleasantries, he leaned forward and asked excitedly. "Robert, would you like to meet Frederick Douglass?"

Robert laughed cheerfully. "You know how much I'd like that! Why, is he here?"

"I saw him yesterday and told him you wanted to meet him. He wants to meet you as well. Let's do it tomorrow."

It was arranged and Frederick Douglass seemed delighted to see them. He told Robert, "Finally, I am meeting the famous Captain Robert Smalls."

My husband could hardly speak. "Sir, I've read everything I could find that you've written. The pleasure is all mine."

The three men found they had a great deal in common, particularly in regard to the rights of the Negroes and their influx into the Union. All three agreed that more Negroes should join the Union's cause in fighting the war.

"And we must be founders, and sponsors, of institutions of higher learning," added Mr. Douglass. "Captain Smalls, I know you've been working on that in Beaufort, and we have to continue widening our approach."

Robert told me there was disagreement on only one issue. While Rev. French and Robert supported President Lincoln for re-election, Mr. Douglass boldly declared that he could not.

"I don't believe he's gone far enough in support of the Negro. The Emancipation was a large step, but more must be done."

Reverend French and I remained silent and contemplated his statement. Finally, I asked him.

"Who will you vote for?"

"I shall support General John C. Fremont," he answered quietly. "He will support blacks."

They continued to enjoy their dinner, spoke of other local concerns and then departed. Robert considered that evening to be one of the best nights of his life.

~

Robert had coaxed me and finally insisted that I become more literate than I was. He found me a tutor. She and I liked each other, and I happily studied and learned to read and write fairly well. I became so excited about this new skill and wanted to read everything I could find. I'm grateful that my husband and daughter never stopped encouraging me to better myself. Being literate is truly a new form of freedom.

One of the last events Robert attended in Philadelphia was a celebration at National Hall, on December 7, in honor of the emancipation of eighty-seven thousand African Americans in Maryland.

President Lincoln's *Emancipation Proclamation* had officially freed enslaved blacks in states that had seceded, but did not free slaves in Maryland, Delaware, Missouri and Kentucky. Many African Americans were confused about their status. In September of 1864, delegates to Maryland's constitutional convention had approved a constitution that abolished slavery. The following month these same voters held a referendum on the Constitution, where they allowed the soldiers in the field to vote as well. This vote was very close and probably would have been defeated without the soldiers' votes. With this, Maryland became the first "border state" to end slavery. This went into effect on November 1, seven days before President Lincoln was re-elected.

My husband, Robert Smalls, was an honored guest at the celebration in National Hall, and was seated on the stage with the speakers. When his valor in seizing *The Planter* was presented, he received a standing ovation. Two years after the escape, his heroism was still recognized and celebrated. Wherever Robert went, he captured the people's hearts.

While we awaited Robert's return to Port Royal, Savannah had fallen to the Union at the hands of Maj. Gen. William Tecumseh Sherman. This victory came at the end of his *March to the Sea*. Sixty thousand troops traversed a three hundred mile march from Atlanta to Savannah. His troops destroyed bridges, pillaged farms and burned plantations. Most of Georgia was left in ruins.

Thousands of slaves abandoned the plantations along the way and followed Sherman's troops. Although some were seeking freedom, the majority were desperately looking for shelter and food. Sherman and his troops were not pleased, and felt encumbered by the slaves. Only a few slaves were able to contribute as cooks or laborers, and others were told to fend for themselves. It was a very emotional time for them. Most of us did what we could for them, but it wasn't enough.

On Christmas night, the night after my husband returned home, seven hundred weak, cold and famished African Americans arrived in Beaufort. Brig. Gen. Saxton described them "in a state of misery which would have moved to pity a heart of stone." He was struggling to give fifteen thousand African Americans rations, clothing and housing.

I wept in Robert's arms when I fully realized the tremendous plight of the homeless.

Robert held me as his solemn eyes focused on mine. "Sugar, we will give what we can, but we cannot resolve this situation," he said, despondently. "Remember when I explained to you why we had to risk everything to escape on *The Planter*? If we had not, we would be enslaved in the city and suffering these depravations felt by so many others in the South."

Finally, General Saxton asked the military and the "good men and women" of the North for help. The answer he received was: "We do not have the resources to help you." Saxton replied: "Unless the charity of the North comes speedily to the rescue, they will die by the hundreds from exposure and disease."

Sadly, so many of them did. Laura M. Towne, the Philadelphia teacher who started the Penn School in 1862, and a friend of Charlotte Forten, explained the terrible dilemma in her local newspaper article. *The poor Negroes die as fast as ever. The children are all emaciated to the last degree and have such violent coughs and dysenteries that few can survive. It is frightful to see such suffering among children.*

Secretary of War Stanton, now in poor health himself, traveled to Savannah to meet with General Sherman. They spoke about the Negroes' predicament and how to proceed. Secretary Stanton wanted to meet with local black leaders and hear their concerns and requests. In January of 1865, they met with twenty black religious leaders—mostly Baptist and Methodist ministers—at Sherman's headquarters. Fifteen of them were born as slaves.

Secretary Stanton asked them a total of twelve questions, and later remarked how impressed he was with the men's wisdom. Returning to Washington, D.C., he told President Lincoln he could not have received better answers if he had questioned the president's cabinet.

The consensus was that the former slaves wanted land. "We want to be placed on land until we are able to buy it and make it our own." They were asked if they wanted to live with whites or in a separate community. The majority wanted to live separately, and stated as a group: "We prefer to live by ourselves, for there is a prejudice against us in the South that will take years to overcome."

Four days after the meeting, General Sherman issued "Special Field Order 15." The order set aside several areas for the settlement of the Negroes. These areas were on coastal lands, stretching from Charleston, South Carolina to northern Florida, "for the settlement of the Negroes now made free by the acts of war and by the proclamation of the President of the United States."

Each family was given "a plot of not more than forty acres of tillable ground." They were given possessory titles (they owned the land but could not produce titles to prove it) and would be protected by the military authorities until they could protect themselves or until Congress could regulate their title.

The army would give them mules that were no longer fit for military work, which led to the phrase "40 acres and a mule." Any property already sold in the earlier tax sales was not affected. The order also declared: *No white person whatsoever, unless military officers and soldiers detailed for duty, will be permitted to reside; and the sole and exclusive management of affairs will be left to the freed people themselves.*

Sherman's order was quickly circulated, and within six months forty-thousand African Americans were living on the land. Some of the settlements were in Beaufort County. Sherman and Saxton asked Robert to assist in transporting these families from Savannah to their new homes. On February 1, 1865, he entered into a contract with the U.S. Army "for vitalizing and manning the U.S. steamer *The Planter* for the purpose of carrying out this mission." My husband was given $1,937 to accomplish this assignment.

SEVENTEEN
Elizabeth

Charleston was defeated and crushed by the Union. Daddy was called on to transport two black regiments to occupy the city. On March 18, 1865, he proudly entered the city aboard *The Planter*, with General Rufus Saxton at his side.

"General, I haven't been here since my last voyage in May of 1862," Daddy reminisced, as they looked around and saw the heavy toll the war had taken on Charleston. It was far different from the place he had left only three years before.

"Captain Smalls, it must be heartbreaking for you to see such ruin and devastation," consoled the General. "So much of your life was spent here…so many memories."

My father pointed skyward, shaking his head in sadness. "Look at the steeple of St. Michael's. It's been ruined by shells." Together they searched for the stable on East Bay where he and Mama had lived as a newly married couple, but it was gone.

During their walk around the dock area, some of his friends came by. My father introduced General Saxton to these men and then introduced him to John Simmons—the sail maker and a major builder of *The Planter*—who hurried over to enfold Daddy in a strong embrace.

"This man gave me my first job on the dock, and taught me enough to eventually become captain," Daddy told General Saxton with a broad grin.

He explained to him about the "dock friends" connection as others came over to welcome Daddy home. "These gentlemen made *The Planter*, and I put the polish on her," he chuckled.

Some African Americans also appeared, having heard that Captain Smalls and *The Planter* were in town. Daddy enjoyed listening to their gratitude for their liberation. Some of them even gave him the credit. He talked with them for several hours, while General Saxton and the other officials walked around the city doing their inspections.

My father saw John Ferguson, the former owner of *The Planter*, standing a few meters away. John offered him a slight nod, but neither man approached the other. When Captain Smalls seized the ship, most of the blame fell on the owner, Ferguson, and not on the white officers who had left the vessel in the care of the enslaved crew. Daddy's escape had cost Mr. Ferguson the leasing fees he had previously received from the Confederacy.

I often think back on Daddy's impact on this city. It took the war to prove his strength and heroism. He wore that heroism well, and was worshiped by blacks and respected by whites in many parts of the country. Yet he remained his kind, soft-spoken self.

The war basically ended on April 9, 1865. Secretary Stanton ordered a national salute to be fired at noon on April 14, 1865, exactly four years to the day that the Confederate flag was struck down. Daddy and his crew learned they would be included in this honorable event. This ceremonial raising of the Union flag over Fort Sumter was in honor of its restoration. Daddy would pilot *The Planter*, and nine other steamers would carry soldiers and civilians from Charleston to Fort Sumter to participate in this historic event. President Lincoln was invited to attend, and

Daddy was very excited to introduce him to his southern world. He knew the president would ride on *The Planter*, and he, Captain Smalls, would proudly pilot the ship.

President Lincoln, trying to prepare the nation for the future, gave his second inaugural address in the East Portico at the U.S. Capital. Speaking to forty thousand onlookers, he encouraged reconciliation in that speech. He only spoke seven minutes, but he named the institution of slavery as the cause of the war and called it a national debt created by the "bondmen's 250 years of unrequited toil." The amendment to abolish slavery was passed by the House and the Senate, and was ready to be ratified by the states. In his closing remarks, the president called for the country to reunite "with malice toward none; with charity for all."

President Lincoln seriously considered attending the ceremony at Fort Sumter, but his advisors discouraged him due to safety concerns. Given this advice, the president stayed in Washington.

On the day of the event, Captain Smalls loaded up his ship with as many people as he could fit in: freedmen, old men, middle-aged men and women, cadaverous and ragged beings in tattered clothing, young boys and girls filled with excitement, etc. They huddled together, hung over gunwales, doubled up in corners, and shouted with glee, showing their support and gratitude to the Union. The white-haired men's faces lit up with deep joy. Middle-aged women of every color were decorated with turbans and bandanas of flashy colors. Daddy sat above them at the wheel, a prince among them, self-possessed and proud, and directing orders to the helmsman in ringing tones of command.

General Robert Anderson, the man who had lowered the American flag in defeat four years ago, stepped forward to speak. "After four long years of bloody war, and at

President Lincoln's request, I am restoring this dear flag to its proper place. This flag floats here today during peace. I thank God that I have lived to see this day and am able to perform this duty to my country. Glory to God in the highest! Peace on earth and good will toward men!"

All the surrounding forts—Forts Moultrie, Pinckney, Ripley, Putnam, Johnson, Cumming's Point, and Battery Bee—answered in jubilation. The Naval vessels in the harbor gave a thunderous national signal as they fired twenty-one gun salutes. Flags flew from public and private buildings throughout the city.

Reverend Henry Ward Beecher, an eloquent abolitionist, had commissioned a ship to bring his Brooklyn congregation with him to celebrate. "It is not the same flag!" he shouted. "When it went down four years ago, four million people had no flag. Today it rises and four million people cry out, *'Behold our flag!' No more slavery!*"

As soon as the flag reached its full height on the flagpole, one hundred guns from Fort Sumter fired in salute. A band erupted into national songs, and the forts, batteries and vessels in the harbor fired their own salutations until the air was filled with smoke.

Daddy described it all to me in great detail, and I wrote it down for him as a keepsake. He told me that when he saw the American flag flying over Fort Sumter, the place where the war that led to his freedom had begun, he fell to his knees, overcome by a powerful sense of patriotism.

There was a gathering at the Zion Presbyterian Church the following morning. Although it was the largest church in the city, it was filled beyond capacity, leaving many standing outside. William Lloyd Garrison was carried to the pulpit on men's shoulders. His address was commanding, but often overwhelmed by the singing, shouting, crying and cheering.

Charleston, Beaufort and all the rest of the state did not learn for four days about the tragic news in the north. On the night of the day we celebrated victory on Fort Sumter, President Lincoln was assassinated in Ford's Theatre in Washington, D. C.

When Daddy heard the news, he wept. "If only they had allowed him to come here, that would never have happened." He told our family he felt like he'd lost a family member. "He meant so much to me and everyone who knew him," he said. "Lord have mercy on us all."

The nation was grief-stricken. So many African Americans, including Daddy and his friends, saw him as their liberator. Mama told me that she and Daddy felt that by declaring his support for the right of blacks to vote, he had made a bold step in empowering them. And Daddy's hero and friend, Frederick Douglass, made a similar statement several months later.

> *The colored people believed in Abraham Lincoln thoroughly, even when, at times, he seemed to smite them. They saw him not in regard to certain words, which may have occasionally dropped from him, but they believed in him as a whole, in his great statesmanship and manhood. They saw themselves being gradually lifted to freedom; under his rule they saw millions of their brethren declared free.*

With Lincoln gone, the task of Reconstruction fell to President Andrew Johnson, a former slaveholder from Tennessee, who believed "white men alone must manage the South." My parents told me they could foresee the strife, confusion and hostility that would plague the country, at the time the government brought the seceded states back into the Union and tried to safeguard the rights of African Americans.

Daddy's final trip on *The Planter* was a significant sentimental journey. He quietly piloted her to the new Freedmen's Bureau to help out with the resettlement of war refugees. She was disarmed, after which my father took her to Baltimore to be sold on the commercial market. He left her there and rode the train home, covering his face with his hat when the tears began to fall. Fortunately he wasn't recognized. By the time he reached home, he had accepted the fate of his beloved vessel.

~

Religion was an important part of the Smalls' family life during the post-Civil War years. When emancipation began, the Baptist religion was the choice of the family. When the Union forces arrived in Beaufort in November of 1861, Gramma Lydia was an active member of the Baptist Church of Beaufort. After the white people fled, she joined her black friends for Sunday services at the Tabernacle. In 1863, the Tabernacle Baptist Church was officially established with its own pastor. Lydia continued worshiping there and took us with her.

Daddy was too busy with military duties to join us in church until 1865, when the white families returned to Beaufort. He joined and became a chief financial supporter of the First African Baptist Church of Beaufort, just a short walk from our home. Mama told me that Daddy was their primary supporter and gave enough money to hold the mortgage so the church could be bought from the Beaufort Baptist Church. He also became associated with the Brick Baptist Church on St. Helena Island, which was affiliated with the Penn School, where I studied.

I once asked Daddy where he learned so much about management skills if he never attended school.

"Well, my dear Lizzie, I watched Henry McKee when I was still a lad, and asked him questions. Then I looked around me and listened during the time I worked on the docks in Charleston. Those experiences taught me a lot. That's when I bought my first little store, which did very well." He gave me a mischievous grin. "I believe you'll become quite the businesswomen yourself one day, which will make your mother and me very proud."

Daddy believed that blacks should own and operate business enterprises. He showed them how when he bought several businesses on Carteret Street, and allowed them to invest with him, offering shares in the general store he purchased. He also went into business with a former soldier in the South Carolina black regiment, and a few other black men. They called their business *The Star Spangled Banner Association,* and purchased a store and a steamboat, to be commanded by Daddy. They raised $20,000 from local Beaufort residents in shares ranging from $15 to $200.

"Sadly, Lizzie, that ship ran aground on Johns Island, when another wheelman was piloting her. We had a mortgage of $10,000 on her, and lost that and more. Fortunately, my store was doing very well," he chuckled, shrugging his shoulders.

During the next few years, Daddy purchased several houses in our neighborhood that he used for rental income and to house relatives. My sister and I (and later our little brother Willie) learned from his example, but didn't follow through with that knowledge until much later in life.

EIGHTEEN

Robert

I was sick in May, June and the beginning of July of 1865. I must have contracted malaria while loading and unloading cotton onto *The Planter*. Just when I felt I was well enough to go out, I came down with a different illness in July, and the doctors sent me back to bed in Beaufort for almost a month. Mama, Hannah and a nurse took care of me, and Elizabeth helped them after she returned from school. She was also a wonderful big sister to Sarah, and gave her mother a little time for herself in the afternoon.

I tried to keep up with the national news, and listened closely to any information about President Johnson's Reconstruction Plan. Occasionally, we'd talk about this in the evening, or at the supper table when I was feeling better. My mother and Hannah brought newspapers and shared local gossip to keep me informed.

"Even though President Johnson freed his slaves, he continues to say blacks are inferior to whites!" I grumbled late one afternoon, tossing the paper aside. "Who does..."

Hannah interrupted, "But Robert, he's saying the end of slavery is necessary. Are those just words that he thinks will help his political career?"

"That's how it sounds to me," I muttered, confused about my mindset regarding his sincerity.

Then I answered Hannah's question. "Here they quote him during a speech to a black audience, after President

Lincoln chose Johnson to be his vice president. *I will indeed be your Moses and lead you through the Red Sea of war and bondage to a fairer future of liberty and peace.* What has he done about that?"

President Johnson answered my question through his actions, six weeks after President Lincoln's death. He revealed his plans for Reconstruction, by giving amnesty to former Confederates who had pledged to defend the Constitution and support emancipation. All property (except slaves) would be returned to those who took the oath.

But as I learned more, I realized his Amnesty Proclamation had many restrictions. The Southerners who owned more than $20,000 in taxable property would have to apply directly to the president for his pardon. So would most of the Confederate officials.

"Good God, why do they have to appeal to him?" I cried out in frustration. "He's always hated the Southerners who have money, even though he grew up in Tennessee!"

President Johnson pardoned seven thousand planters, allowing *the planter elite* to regain political control in the South. The radical Republicans in Congress were livid.

His second proclamation was directed at the black population, although he concealed his intent with fancy words. He named a provisional governor for North Carolina, and told him to call a convention to organize a new state constitution. In President Johnson's words: *Only those men who had been eligible to vote before the state seceded and who had taken the loyalty oath would be allowed to elect the delegates to the convention.*

"He's totally excluding Negroes!" I shouted out. There were too many things that upset me about this new president.

Hannah pointed out the information to me when she found it in our local newspaper, partially hidden under local news. Hannah had recently learned to read and enjoyed using her new skill. Lizzie helped her when she could, and sometimes I took my free time to work with her as well. The girls did their "school work" in the evening. We've become a proud family of three literates, and now are attempting to convince my mother, Lydia, to work with Hannah's tutor to make it four.

Then the president made his proclamations for South Carolina. Benjamin F. Perry, a Unionist and a racist, would be the provisional governor. I had already labeled him a racist because of his quote: *"The African has been, in all ages, a savage or a slave. God created him inferior to the white man in form, color, and intellect, and no legislation or culture can make him his equal."*

Perhaps it took me so long to convalesce from my illnesses because I was so angry. The one thing that helped me was that the blacks were making it clear that the old ways were gone now. I heard them telling the whites, "We own this land now. Put it out of your head that it will ever be yours again."

Though unopposed, President Johnson pushed his policies, because Congress was in recess and wouldn't reconvene until early December. I knew this was deliberate timing.

That spring many Union troops were sent to Charleston from Beaufort and Hilton Head, depriving former slaves of the protection they had previously been offered. At the same time, a good number of white residents were returning to reclaim their homes and other property, as they had been doing in Charleston.

To us, the black population, the future looked threatening and bleak.

~

When the white residents of Beaufort returned in 1865, the land conflicts began. The Negroes who had received land as a result of General Sherman's Special Field Orders clashed with the returning white families, who said the land was theirs. My home on Prince Street wasn't affected at this time, although eventually I would have to take my case to the U.S. Supreme Court in order to keep it.

To help resolve this, a long-time abolitionist, Gen. Oliver O. Howard, was appointed commissioner of the new Freedmen's Bureau in May 1865. This agency provided medical care, education, food, clothing, and legal assistance to former slaves and poor whites. It also was tasked with distributing abandoned land in the Sea Islands, including those lands designated under Sherman's Special Field Orders, No. 15.

General Saxton was chosen as the assistant commissioner for both South Carolina and Georgia, and quickly started helping the African Americans get land. But on September 12, the White House issued a new order: *all who had taken the loyalty oath and had been pardoned will be eligible to reclaim their lands (not including those sold in the direct tax sale).*

I was furious with this rash decision. "So now the long-term dream of many newly-freed African Americans to own their own property has suddenly evaporated! This is not what President Lincoln wanted!"

Hannah agreed. "Oh Sugar, this will give no more protection to our people. But let's wait to see what happens when Congress reconvenes in December."

And then my old friend, Admiral Samuel Du Pont, died unexpectedly on June 23. This was a personal loss and it deeply saddened me. He had hired me as a pilot, made sure my crew received the prize money for taking *The Planter,* and supported Rev. French's and my trip to Washington to meet President Lincoln. He believed in me and in our people. In such a short period of time, I had lost too many friends.

I started considering politics as an option. Because I was so upset about what Washington D.C. was doing, I seriously contemplated helping by "being the solution." After the Constitutional Convention of South Carolina, whose delegates were mostly former Confederates, I listened to the comments people made about returning to the Union. President Johnson had listed several requirements to rejoin. He said that each state had to nullify the Ordinance of Secession and abolish slavery. Each state had to repudiate the Confederacy's debt.

On September 28, the delegates of this convention sent the president the results. They had repealed the Ordinance of Secession, abolished slavery, and "directed a commission to submit a code to the Legislature for the protection of the colored population."

Unfortunately, these were only "part realities." They did not mention repudiating the Confederate debt. They repealed, rather than nullified, the Ordinance of Secession (rescinded it instead of making it illegal), and they sent the "repudiation of slavery" to the U.S. authorities, and not to the state.

This newly-formed state legislature created a separate set of laws for blacks, called *The Black Codes*. This was an attempt to preserve slavery and prohibited everything from intermarriages between blacks and whites to blacks' owning non-hunting firearms and participating in militia service. They even redefined the terms of servants and master.

Naturally, the black population protested. Still, these *Black Codes* were enacted in December.

My friends, family and I were in agreement: the North may have won the war, but the nation was still doing its best to reinstate slavery.

And then, in an act that completely confused everyone, the president declared that Reconstruction was completed in December of 1865. Republicans were furious and refused to recognize the new state government. In December of 1865, Georgia became the twenty-seventh of thirty-six states to abolish slavery by ratifying the 13th Amendment.

"My friend Frederick Douglass is a prophet," I told my family that evening, reading his quote in the newspaper. He said: *Slavery is not abolished until the black man has the ballot. While the Legislatures of the South retain the right to pass laws making any discrimination between black and white, slavery still lives there.*

My dear Hannah smiled and answered, "Amen."

NINETEEN
Elizabeth

By the time I was eight years old, I could already read at an adult level. Miss Forten wanted her students to read and write early and often. Her emphasis was on sending us to other "worlds" through the written word, and we were eager learners. Before I reached my twelfth birthday, Miss Forten was discussing with my parents which and where my next school should be. She recommended that I go north to attend the *West Newton English and Classical School*, a private school in West Newton, Massachusetts.

They decided to talk this over with me at the beginning of my final year at the *Penn School*. I think they wanted to have time to convince me before the acceptance deadline came.

I was a bit reluctant when they told me what they knew about the school and West Newton. "I think I would like that, but it's so far away from you two and Sarah."

Mama nodded, smiling. "Lizzie, you'll have such unique and interesting experiences, and you'll be able to meet new people with different ideas. We'll visit you, and you'll come home for the holidays."

Daddy was delighted with the idea of the school, but seemed troubled that I would be living so far away. The three of us talked this through many times before we made our decision.

It turned out that I did attend that school, also called the *Allen School*. It was founded in 1854 by Nathaniel Topliff Allen—a strong advocate of women's suffrage, the abolition of slavery, and temperance. One interesting feature about the school was that the student body was racially integrated and co-educational, which was very progressive at the time. Also, my favorite subject, gymnastics, was included as part of the courses offered, which was an academic first.

Although it was co-educational, there were more females than males attending. I think that's because it was referred to as a "finishing school." Finishing schools are created to teach social graces and upper-class cultural rituals. Etiquette is stressed there, but so are the academic subjects. Young men benefited from learning leadership skills, career planning and communication. Everyone benefited by acquiring a refined way of conducting themselves.

I was a curious child with a huge imagination. From the first time they brought it up, I was eager about the possibility of going to school in the north. Throughout my childhood, both of my parents encouraged me to participate in adult conversations and listen to wise and knowledgeable people. "You are a smart girl Lizzie, and it's important to use your opportunities to your advantage," Mama often said.

The school's coursework included reading, spelling, arithmetic, geography, geology and bookkeeping. Mr. Allen required all students to keep daily journals that were critiqued every two weeks. We were encouraged to comment in detail on what we liked and disliked about any subject, including politics and later, the reconstruction period. Writing became my leisure pursuit.

I befriended girls and boys from many parts of the world. During the five years I was enrolled there, students came from Europe, Central and South America,

Cuba, Puerto Rico, Jamaica, Nassau, Japan, the United States and other countries. Many of the teachers were Mr. Allen's relatives: cousins, uncles, brothers, nieces and three daughters. Other relatives and close friends offered their homes for student lodging. Luckily, I lived with one of those families.

I remember when the whites returned to Beaufort after the war. They said they were shocked that they weren't subjected to anger, hostility or resentment from the black population. Thomas Elliot, a planter friend of my father, told him that his former slaves received him with universal kindness and a friendly attitude.

"Is that because they were afraid President Johnson would send them back into slavery?" wondered my Gramma Lydia.

"Or, is it their kindness and compassion? They might feel they can now help those who once held so much power over them," suggested Daddy.

I absorbed those conversations and formed my own opinions, even at a young age. I believed it depended on the treatment they were given while they were enslaved. My parents are a good example of those who treated whites well. Even as slaves, they gave and received kindness from whites and blacks alike.

We watched silently and were pleased to see Negroes offering to lend their former owners money, food and shelter, even though they were facing their own struggles.

One day, Daddy saw a dirty man, who appeared to be hungry, sitting on the front porch of a store. He recognized him as Henry McKee's cousin.

"Well, hello, my friend!" Daddy's warm greeting brought a smile to the man's face.

"Robert Smalls, right?" the man asked, rubbing his eyes.

"Yes, Sir. It is nice to see you again." He waited a beat, and then walked over to shake his hand. "Do you mind if I give you a small piece of advice?"

The man studied Daddy with a puzzled expression.

Daddy explained, "That Confederate jacket you're wearing. It could put you in danger. Five regiments of black troops are in town today to be paid and you could attract their attention with that gray jacket."

The man appeared somewhat feeble as he slowly shifted in his chair. "Thank you for your advice, Captain Smalls," he said.

Daddy crouched down and smiled at him. "Come with me, Sir. Let's replace the coat." Daddy took him to a friend's store and bought him a new suit to wear.

Another story illustrating Daddy's kindness touches my heart whenever I think about it. Mama told me that during the final months of 1875, Daddy learned that Henry McKee's widow, Jane, and some of her children were living in a crowded apartment in Charleston. He went to visit them, and after some conversation, asked Mrs. McKee if they might prefer to live in a larger space—in his house in Beaufort—the same one that once belonged to the McKees and where their children grew up. After considering this idea for a few weeks, they accepted his offer. Daddy paid their railroad fare, and they moved in.

At this point, Mama laughed. "But they would not take their meals with us. We enjoyed their presence and conversation during the day as friends, but when the mealtimes came around, they asked to be served at a different table."

"Well, Mama, perhaps they could only accept pieces of your hospitality," I offered.

She nodded. "It's what the Lord had in mind all along, I believe. And it worked well for all of us."

~

In Beaufort County, slaves had been free since November, 1861, and the number of free blacks had increased greatly after Sherman's arrival at the coast. After the war, South Carolina had a population of approximately 400,000 blacks and 275,000 whites. Charleston had about 17,000 blacks, while Beaufort County towns, plantations and military camps had about 30,000. Blacks were concentrated on the coast—the Low Country—and made up 83% of the residents.

Other than their freedom, blacks had gained little from the war. Most saw themselves as victims of the Union army's scorched earth policies. Still, they did not seek vengeance against their former masters, as so many expected them to do. Nearly all of them were poorer than they were during slavery. Our family understood how fortunate we were.

This realization of deprivation pained our family and many others. We wanted to work together, but were leery of our leaders in Washington, D.C. We heard that the federal government was struggling to find a policy for the reconstruction of the South.

One of the problems was that black citizens were needed for their labor. White leaders had to find ways to get around the circumstance of defeat and keep blacks subjugated and working. Northerners were also confused about how to treat the blacks. After emancipation, the reality of economic and social integration became an immediate consideration. President Lincoln's untimely death left his plans unfinished. One advantage for the freed slaves in South Carolina was the test case of the Sea Islands, where blacks had already been the focus of a society's reconstruction for nearly four years.

But protection, by government agents and Freedmen's Aid Societies, fell short of levels reached under slavery. Rice and cotton growing did not recover from wartime neglect of irrigation and flood control infrastructure. Many ex-slaves learned to make their living by hiring themselves out to landowners for pay or shares. This new system of bondage evolved in many cases.

The federal government was struggling with a policy for reconstructing the country. In 1863, President Lincoln had proposed to allow the rebel states to return to their former status when 10% of the 1860 voters accepted abolition. He would then have pardoned them (after the Confederates signed the Loyalty Oath), and restored their rights of citizenship and property, minus their slaves.

But the new President Johnson appeared to be prejudiced in both his statements and actions. In his message to Congress in 1867, he said: "Blacks have shown less capacity for government than any other race of people. No independent government of any form has been successful in their hands." He favored state's rights and didn't believe the federal government should dictate terms of reconstruction.

In May of 1865, he appointed Benjamin Perry, a former Unionist who served in the South Carolina legislature during the war, as provisional governor. Then he directed Perry to call a constitutional convention with the intent of restoring the state to the Union. An election to choose delegates to the convention was called on September 13, 1865.

Voting was restricted to those who were eligible to vote in 1860, so no blacks could participate.

This convention was calculated to fail. President Johnson pardoned 845 otherwise disqualified rebels before the convention convened. These delegates were old-guard—former representatives, legislators, Confederate officers—who voted to abolish slavery and nullify secession, but would not accept the third point: repudiation of Confederate debts. And the final insult was—they refused to fly the American flag over the convention site.

Congress declined to endorse most of Johnson's actions and did not seat senators and representatives-elect. The Black Code laws were of great concern to the Congress, and so was the action taken by the president of pardoning ex-Confederates, with little regard for the adverse effects on the Sea Island blacks. President Johnson spoke about returning the once-abandoned properties the blacks now occupied back over to the pardoned rebels.

The lands at issue were those used for resettlement of refugee blacks under Sherman's Field Order No. 15. The blacks thought they were getting a permanent title, but Sherman stated he intended to make "temporary provisions for the freedmen and their families during the rest of the war."

In 1866, Congress's dissatisfaction with Johnson's reconstruction policies, and the failure to understand them, came to light in new legislation and constitutional amendments, designed to give blacks equal rights. Congress's real concern was the political control over the South so as to keep Republican majorities in the Senate and House of Representatives. New amendments were passed, such as the Fourteenth Amendment, defining citizenship and expanding federal protection of rights limited by a state.

My Daddy was not directly involved in making these changes. His political profile was low, yet he continued working and speaking to groups when invited. He also purchased a small store in Beaufort and a steamboat. One article written during this time describes him kindly. "*Small's rise to political importance during the Reconstruction was inevitable. He was good-humored, intelligent, fluent and self-possessed.*" Another observer noted: "*He is now in independent circumstances, and is regarded by all the other Negroes as immensely rich, and decidedly the smartest colored man in South Carolina. He is able to give bread to half the bank presidents and brokers of Broad Street in Charleston.*"

I was studying up north during most of this time and depended on my visits and their letters to understand how my family was living during these trying times. I knew little about the every-day problems in the South while I was away. Yet, my pride in my family remained strong and secure, and I believed we would make it in spite of these trials.

TWENTY
Robert

Some believe I was the founder of the South Carolina Republican party. I wasn't alone. About eight of us formed a small group in 1867, holding meetings and discussions about how to improve conditions for the Sea Island blacks. We called ourselves the *Beaufort Republican Club*. They asked me to be their leader, and with a smile and a handshake, the party was created.

I spoke at the first meeting and evoked the memory of President Lincoln, the Great Emancipator. *"We, as receivers of the Emancipator's gift of grace, must do everything in our power to spread, cultivate and maintain that gift in this world and amongst the future generations."* That year we started a school for African American children in Beaufort. Prior to the war we had used the same buildings to school our black children. We later learned that the government returned the buildings to their former white owners.

I served as a delegate at several Republican National Conventions, and was selected to participate in the South Carolina Republican State Convention of 1868. My main project was to provide free, compulsory schooling available to all of South Carolina's children. We worked hard on this task, and were successful almost immediately. Those schools continued for years.

That same year, I was elected to the South Carolina House of Representatives. I felt a strong need to be there, where I knew my voice was crucial, especially for introducing bills. Two of the bills I introduced were a Homestead Act and a Civil Rights bill. I'm happy to say that our hard work pushed the Civil Rights bill into law.

My local political success led to my election as one of the first African American members of Congress. I ultimately served five terms in the U.S. House of Representatives. I still feel a sense of wonder and gratitude when I think about my humble birth and childhood. I didn't know how to read and write until I passed age twenty. After that, I served in Washington almost continuously from 1875 to 1887.

I give thanks to God who prepared me to do this work. My ability to speak English and Gullah helped me tremendously. The Sea Island blacks told me I had a new title: "King of Beaufort County"—a title given to me by my political opponents, and one I proudly claimed.

In 1870, luck was again on my side. Jonathan Jasper Wright was elected judge of the South Carolina Supreme Court, and I was chosen to fill his unexpired term in the state Senate. I remained there even after I won the 1872 election against W.J. Whipper.

I truly enjoyed my time as a senator. I love to debate, and I believe I sharpened my skills during this term. I served on the Finance Committee and was chairman of the Public Printing Committee.

Around this time, I decided to form a local marching brass band. Our group of musicians became very popular in Beaufort, and turned up at all local and state celebrations. Since I held a high position in the militia, I dressed in my military uniform and provided similar uniforms for my band members. We called ourselves the Allen Brass Band, and played the most raucous Negro music in the liveliest fashion. Our crowds responded by clapping, dancing and swaying, transported by the rhythm. Beaufort had never seen anything like this, and both the blacks and the whites were delighted. I usually led them, bouncing and smiling and singing with exuberance.

In 1872, I was a delegate to the National Republican Convention. It was held in Philadelphia, and we nominated the incumbent President Grant for re-election. I was elected vice-president of the South Carolina Republican Party at its 1872 state convention.

In 1873, I was appointed lieutenant colonel of the Third Regiment, South Carolina State Militia. I thought I had reached my ultimate military dream, but God had other plans. I was later promoted to brigadier general of the Second Brigade, South Carolina State Militia. And soon after, they promoted me to major general of the Second Division, South Carolina State Militia. I held that position until 1877, when the Democrats took control of the state government.

I worked hard and became a leader in Reconstruction politics. In 1874, I was elected to the United States House of Representatives, where I served two terms from 1875 to 1879. From 1882 to 1883, I represented South Carolina's 5th congressional district in the House. Then, our state legislature gerrymandered the district boundaries, thereby incorporating Beaufort and other heavily African-American coastal areas into South Carolina's 7th congressional district. This provided other nearby districts substantial white majorities. To summarize, I was elected from the 7th district and served from 1884 to 1887. I was the second-longest serving African American member of Congress (behind Joseph Rainey), until the mid-20th century.

During the time I held these political positions, the

conservative Southern Bourbon Democrats used violence and election fraud to regain control of the state legislature. They hoped to link me to Republican corruption, deflecting attention from their own misdeeds. The conservative Democrats tried to defame me and delay my taking the congressional seat, while President Grant's Democrat opponent contested the election.

They were so ruthless that they devised a plan, using me, to help them control the state legislature. I was charged and convicted of accepting a bribe five years earlier (1872) in connection with the awarding of a printing contract. My charge was accepting a $5,000 bribe while I was a state senator. The evidence was weak and was offered by a convicted felon, who received immunity in exchange for his testimony.

I spent three days in jail and was then released, pending appeal. I returned to Congress, ashamed and humiliated, knowing I had been framed. In 1879, the South Carolina Supreme Court finally agreed to hear my appeal.

The appeal process was prejudicial and bigoted. The jury selection had been unfair. I should have been entitled to congressional immunity and my attorney wanted this case transferred to the federal courts. I immediately appealed to the U.S. Supreme Court.

This mock conviction was eventually overturned as part of an agreement where charges were also dropped against white Democrats accused of election fraud. I was very unhappy, because I needed to clear my name. Yet there was nothing I could do, and my reputation suffered for years. This scandal took a huge political toll on me. I was easily defeated by Democrat George Tillman in 1878, and then narrowly lost to him in 1880.

I contested the 1880 result and regained the seat in 1882. Then, in 1884, I was elected to fill the seat in a different district. I was nominated for Senate in 1884, and was defeated by Wade Hampton.

During the time I spent in Congress, I left my mark. I supported racial-integration legislation. I made an impassioned speech in the House of Representatives for an increased pension for the widow of my former Major General, David Hunter. David was well-known for attempting to emancipate African Americans under his charge in 1862, and for creating his own unauthorized regiment of black soldiers. Congress passed the bill, but President Cleveland vetoed it.

I also advised South Carolina's African Americans to refrain from migrating to the northern or mid-western states or to Liberia.

Why am I recording my political history in the written word? Both of my daughters, as well as other people I care about, have asked me that. I tell them it is information they will appreciate in years to come. But it's mostly because I want my life story to be accurate, honest and in my own voice. Some called me the "leading colored delegate" to the 1895 South Carolina Constitutional Convention. Five other African-American politicians and I opposed the dominant Democratic delegates, as they relentlessly allowed the marginalization of the state's African-American citizens to be written into the proposed constitution.

The six of us decided it was necessary to publicize this blatantly discriminatory clause, and we worked very hard on it. Writing together, we composed an article for the *New York World*, and it was published. We fought hard against a great deal of prejudice, but we were outnumbered at the state convention. The constitution that was adopted somehow survived legal challenges, resulting in both the exclusion of African Americans from political participation, and the crippling of the Republican Party throughout South Carolina.

During these trying times, I made a plan to pursue justice for myself. After fighting for years to receive a pension for my wartime service on *The Planter*, I was tired and angry that the government would not consider me a veteran. The government never took into account that when DuPont hired me in 1862, African Americans were not allowed to enlist as *pilots*. As I've explained before, our position was referred to as *"boy"* or *"wheelman."*

I was successful in the outcome of my petition. In 1897, more than thirty years after the war ended, I received $30 monthly as my U.S. Navy pension. That inspired me to try again: I would seek proper compensation for my crew and myself for handing *The Planter* over to the Union forces.

In 1883, a House committee agreed with me that the 1862 appraisal of my ship and its cargo were extremely low. It admitted that a fair 1862 assessment should have been $67,000, instead of the $9,000 given at that time. The federal law that gave money to the crew stipulated that they would receive half the amount of the appraisal: $4584, divided among them. As the crew leader, I would receive the largest sum: $1,500.

Forty years after I seized *The Planter*, Congress chose to award me an additional quantity. $20,000 was suggested, but the Committee on War Claims gave me $5,000. I was grateful and pleased to receive that amount. This finally brought closure for a reasonable reparation during such an important period of my life.

I had to fight to win another well-paid political position. This was the U.S. Customs Collector title for the Port of Beaufort. I was slowly tiring of my congressional career, and its strain on my mind and body.

While in Washington, I had hoped to secure this coveted appointment. I called on my old friend, General Rufus Saxton, to ask for a recommendation. He wrote a letter to President Harrison, describing my wartime service. *Smalls may be regarded as one of the representative men of his race. I am confident that Smalls would perform his duties with fidelity, and advantage to the government.*

I then received an even stronger endorsement from Senator John Sherman, whom I supported for president in the 1888 convention. Sherman wrote: *Though cheated, counted out and persecuted, he is the best type of native Negro in South Carolina. He has more claims upon the consideration of the Administration than anyone else I know. He is able to discharge the duties of the office and has the courage to perform them.*

But a campaign was initiated against me and that appointment. I was accused of deserting the blacks, losing my honor in my state, and putting four Republicans in jail. I countered them with the truth, and won. I was given a temporary commission as Port Collector, effective June 13, 1889. It wasn't permanent, because the Congress was in recess.

A few days after the new Fifty-first Congress convened, my appointment was confirmed on January 10. I accepted the permanent position as Beaufort's Customs Collector, appointed by President Benjamin Harrison, on January 25, 1890.

Captain Robert Smalls *The U.S. Steamer Planter. Courtesy of The Robert Smalls Collection/ Michael B. Moore.*

Robert Smalls in May, 1862, dressed in Captain Relyea's clothes. This was Admiral Du Pont's personal copy. *Courtesy of Hagley Museum and Library.*

Robert Smalls was born into slavery in 1839 in the small town of Beaufort, S.C. *Courtesy of the Library of Congress.*

The Planter in June, 1862. This photograph was taken in Hilton Head, S.C. *Courtesy of Harper's Weekly.*

Drawing of Robert Smalls, about age thirty, as he looked when he was in the S.C. General Assembly. *Courtesy of the African Methodist Episcopal Church Review.*

Hannah Jones Smalls, Robert Small's first wife. Taken from "Robert Smalls and His Descendants." *Courtesy of the Association for the Study of Afro-American Life and History.*

To escape to the Union ships, Robert Smalls had to steam past Fort Sumter, S.C. This is how it looked before the Confederate attack in April 1861. *Courtesy of the Library of Congress.*

Samuel Jones Bampfield, around thirty-three years of age. *Courtesy of The Robert Smalls Collection/Michael B. Moore.*

During the Civil War, a massive fire and 567 days of Union shelling left a third of Charleston, S.C. in ruins. *Courtesy of the Library of Congress.*

Elizabeth Smalls Bampfield in her wedding gown. *Courtesy of The Robert Smalls Collection/Helen Boulware Moore.*

Robert and Hannah Smalls' daughters, Elizabeth and Sarah Smalls. *Courtesy of The Robert Smalls Collection/ Helen Boulware Moore.*

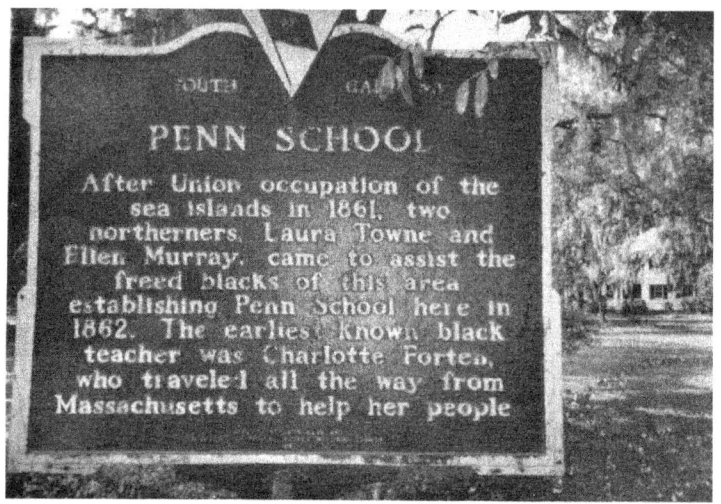

Penn School was established by missionaries for the education of the newly freed slaves. *Courtesy of LyBenson Photography Studios/Rev. Kenneth Hodges, photographer.*

For several years, The Brick Baptist Church, near the Penn School, was used as a classroom of the school. Elizabeth Smalls studied her elementary school education here, and later worked at the school. *Courtesy of LyBenson Photography Studios.*

Residence of Robert Smalls. *Courtesy of The Robert Smalls Collection/Michael B. Moore*

U.S. Representative Robert Smalls about 1889. *Courtesy of the Library of Congress.*

Samuel J. Bampfield and Elizabeth Smalls Bampfield's Beaufort home, where she birthed eleven children. *Courtesy of The Robert Smalls Collection/Michael B. Moore.*

> **The Grandchildren of Robert Smalls**
> (the Children of Elizabeth Lydia Smalls Bampfield
> and Samuel Jones Bampfield).
> front, left to right: Ariana Bampfield Boulware (baby), Albert Barnes Bampfield, and Helen Bampfield Givens (baby). Back, left to right: Elizabeth Bampfield Hall, Sarah Bampfield Meyer (holding baby in lap), Janet Bampfield Davidson, Maria Bampfield Simpson, Julia Bampfield Stinson (holding baby in lap), and Robert Smalls Bampfield.
> *From the Robert Smalls Collection*

Smalls Bampfield Children. *Courtesy of The Robert Smalls Collection/ Michael B. Moore.*

Annie Wiggs Smalls, Robert Smalls' second wife. *Courtesy of The Robert Smalls Collection/ Michael B. Moore.*

Robert Smalls in 1904 or 1905. Robert is pictured as the Beaufort Customs Collector. *Courtesy of The Robert Smalls Collection/Michael B. Moore.*

Robert Smalls 1895. *Courtesy of The Robert Smalls Collection/Michael B. Moore.*

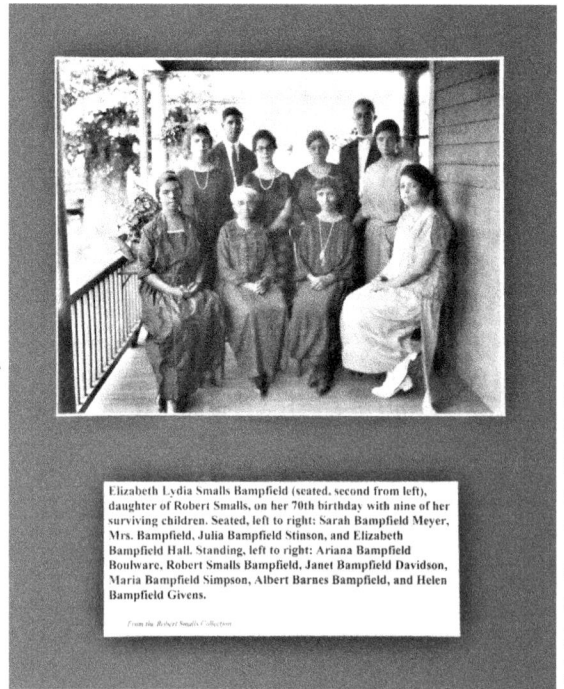

Older Elizabeth (Lizzie) with her family. *Courtesy of The Robert Smalls Collection/ Michael B. Moore.*

Elizabeth Lydia Smalls Bampfield (seated, second from left), daughter of Robert Smalls, on her 70th birthday with nine of her surviving children. Seated, left to right: Sarah Bampfield Meyer, Mrs. Bampfield, Julia Bampfield Stinson, and Elizabeth Bampfield Hall. Standing, left to right: Ariana Bampfield Boulware, Robert Smalls Bampfield, Janet Bampfield Davidson, Maria Bampfield Simpson, Albert Barnes Bampfield, and Helen Bampfield Givens.

Photo taken at Lizzie's 95th Birthday celebration. *Courtesy of The Robert Smalls Collection/Michael B. Moore.*

100th Birthday celebration with her family. *Courtesy of The Robert Smalls Collection/Michael B. Moore*

Headstone for Elizabeth Smalls Bampfield. *Photo taken by author.*

Smalls Memorial, Charleston, S.C. Photo taken by author.

The First African Baptist Church in Beaufort, where Robert Smalls was a member. His funeral was held here. *Photo taken by author.*

TWENTY-ONE

Elizabeth

I will never forget how "free" I felt leaving South Carolina to travel to my new school in Massachusetts. Mama and Sarah accompanied me on the long train ride, and I was already starting to feel independent and even self-sufficient. My little sister was now six years old, and I was almost thirteen. I would miss Sarah and Mama and Daddy too, although he wasn't home most of the time. As we traveled north, I kept myself entertained by staring out the windows and enjoying landscapes I'd never seen before.

Mama reached over to hold my hand. "Are you excited, Lizzie dear? Your life is about to change." She searched my eyes, offering me her gentle smile. "You'll meet new people and learn more about the big world out there." Pausing a moment, she added, "But always remember, we'll be waiting for you at home."

I nodded, squeezing her hand. Hearing her soft voice and feeling her warmth brought a lump to my throat. That small act of tenderness made my eyes mist up.

Sarah climbed out of her seat to move onto my lap. She squeezed me in a big hug. "I don't want you to go, Lizzie. Who will play with me and read me stories? And explain things, and…" She stopped abruptly, her little mouth puckered up in sadness. Tears pooled in her eyes.

My arms circled her waist as I kissed her cheek. "Silly little Sarah. You have so many people who love you. You'll barely know I'm gone."

She shook her head, narrowing her eyes. "Will you be back before your birthday?"

I laughed. "Sarah, I'll probably be home for Christmas, right Mama? And if not, I promise I'll be back before my birthday."

The train trip seemed endless that first time, but I soon learned to count the landmarks as I traveled the route back and forth to West Newton, Pennsylvania. West Newton was a pretty little town, surrounded by ornamental trees and colorful gardens. I immediately noticed the long front porches and prominent bay windows in the houses. The focal point of West Newton was my school, the *West Newton English and Classical School*, also known as the *Allen School*.

I boarded in the large home of one of Mr. Allen's uncles. The food was very good and the accommodations were simple, but comfortable. I studied hard and got high marks. All the students were encouraged to exercise in some form, and since I already loved gymnastics, I took it as a credited class and improved greatly under Miss Rose's guidance and direction.

I quickly made friends with the other students, and in no time at all, found my new best friend. Her name is Renata Giudici and she lives in New York City. We spoke with different accents, had been raised in dissimilar ways (she was of Italian descent), yet we bonded immediately. It was also her first year at the school, and she lived just down the street in another boardinghouse.

Renata loved to sing, and I loved to dance. We were both athletic and found a beautiful little river to swim in and lounge around on warm days. During the colder days we sat before the fire and read. Reading was high on our list of "most enjoyable activities," as were writing and journal keeping. We laughed often, discussed everything we thought about and shared moments of sadness when we needed to. We were very happy living our lives together, and she made everything so much fun.

One of the highlights of this school was its guest speaker program. We were told that Theodore Parker, an American transcendentalist, reformation minister and abolitionist, had visited just last year. Ralph Waldo Emerson, an abolitionist from Boston, spoke three years ago at the *Allen School*. He is a famous poet whose essay "Nature" explains his philosophy of Transcendentalism. All the students, including the new ones, have already read that essay this year. I hoped he would come back while I was still a student there.

I think every one of us was looking forward to meeting and hearing Rebecca Lee Crumpler, the first African American woman to become a physician. She was an alumni of the *Allen School* and returned frequently to speak to the students. I thought it was special that she received her medical degree from the *New England's Female Medical College*. At this point, I was thinking about becoming a doctor. She returned to the *Allen School* during my last year there. I enjoyed meeting her and asking her questions. I even wrote a paper about her.

The five years at the *Allen School* passed by too quickly. Of course I went home for summer breaks, and three times over the Christmas breaks. My parents and sister visited me in West Newton during one Christmas season, and Renata's family opened their home to me for another Christmas. Every summer, before returning to our homes, she and I traveled to other cities and states. These were wonderful educational experiences, just as Mama and Daddy had told me.

On one railroad trip when Daddy accompanied me, he brought up the subject of economic development. "Lizzie, several years ago, knowing you would be traveling by railroad in the future, I decided to get a franchise from the legislature for the Beaufort Railroad Company. Other investors and I felt that it would be essential to this area, and now it is."

"What do you mean, Daddy?" Sometimes his unexpected conversations confused me.

"Well, Joseph Rainey, Alonzo Ransier and others formed the *Enterprise Railroad*, an 18-mile horse-drawn railway. It carried cargo and passengers between the Charleston wharves and inland depots."

I looked into his eyes and grinned. "Is there a "moral" to this story, Daddy?"

He laughed at my precocious remark.

"Yes there is. Except for one white director (newspaper editor, legislator and county treasurer Tim Hurley), the railroad's board of directors was entirely African American."

Daddy was watching me closely. "It's now 1873, and the railroad is completed and providing much needed transportation to our area. During all this time, it has also given work to many blacks and whites. It's helped our area grow tremendously."

I loved to hear stories of how my father reached out and helped others through his kindness and love for his city and country. He did so many things that I knew nothing about, so I enjoyed our conversations where I would eventually learn more about him.

On my first summer vacation back home, I was thirteen years old and the city asked me to read the *Declara-*

tion of Independence from the second-story verandah of a Beaufort store. This reading had become a traditional part of the town's annual Fourth of July celebration, and was usually recited by a man of importance in our city. That year Daddy asked if his daughter could read it. I think it had become a highpoint for our black citizens, since most of the adults in the audience had been enslaved and still couldn't read or write.

I stood proud and unafraid as I read every single word slowly and clearly. Later I was surprised I hadn't felt nervous.

"Well done, my Lizzie," praised Daddy, hugging me closely.

"Oh Daddy, I'm so happy to know that you continue to stress education to our people who still can't read or write." I felt very proud of him and grateful that he had instilled in his family a strong work ethic, love of country, and the belief that we could do anything in life that we chose. His life was the best example of that. Now educated, he made sure his wife and children would continue to receive the best education available, and he followed through on that.

My father was elected a U.S. congressman from Beaufort County in 1874. He arrived in Washington on December 6, 1874, for the opening of the Forty-first Congress. Daddy quickly located a two-bedroom apartment on Second Street, knowing I would be living with him after I graduated from the *Allen School* in the spring. I was very excited to get my first job: secretary and clerk to a U.S. congressman, who happened to be my father.

Daddy didn't waste any time before he introduced a bill requiring the federal government to return unused land to the state that had been confiscated for nonpayment of taxes. The bill passed, and blacks and others could now purchase land cheaply. This was especially important because the blacks owned three-fourths of the land in Beaufort County, and made up 80% of the population and 70% of the registered voters.

Then Daddy learned about the matter of selecting a southern navy base on the Atlantic. He proposed Port Royal, South Carolina, knowing it had all the qualifications. He discovered that two Georgia ports were being considered as final candidates.

Daddy did his research, found enough data to prove that Port Royal was the best location, and quickly submitted a bill to back it up. This bill passed both houses of the Congress. Then he had to get federal money to improve the port and persuaded the navy to allocate $40,000. This bill passed with little debate. Daddy had just given his state a huge economic boost.

Unfortunately, the Hamburg Massacre hardened the blacks' reputation with the Democrats. During a Hamburg, South Carolina centennial celebration by a black militia held on July 4, 1876, their leader—Doc Adams—refused to disband his men so two white farmers could pass by. Threats, harsh words and accusations were shouted out, until Doc Adams finally moved his men aside and allowed the whites passage.

One of the farmers appeared before Judge Rivers the next day, demanding the arrest of Doc Adams. Both Adams and Judge Rivers were black Republican leaders, Union Army veterans and friends. Adams openly criticized the judge for hearing the case, and Judge Rivers cited him for contempt of court, and set his trial date for July 8.

The trial was held in Hamburg, South Carolina, and Doc Adams' militia gathered in town, as well as a large group of white men, known as the *Red Shirts*. This group of armed white men terrorized the blacks by riding day and night, firing into the houses of Republicans and breaking up Republican mass meetings.

Former Confederate General Matthew C. Butler ordered Adams to disarm his men. Then fighting broke out between the militia and the armed *Red Shirts*. Instead of disarming, the militia retreated to their barracks. General Butler went into Augusta, Georgia, and returned with a cannon and hundreds of *Red Shirts* on horses.

The unarmed and outnumbered black militiamen tried to flee, but were followed. Hamburg's black marshal was mortally wounded, and twenty-five of his men were captured. Then one white youth was killed, and in retaliation, five of the captive militiamen were murdered in cold blood. General Butler denied ordering the executions, but excused them nevertheless.

South Carolina's Governor Daniel Chamberlain denounced this massacre and wrote to one correspondent, *"If you can find words to characterize this atrocity and barbarism, your power of language exceeds mine."*

At this point, my father petitioned and received a congressional inquiry. Chamberlain seated a grand jury to investigate, and that jury indicted seven men for murder and also named several dozen accessories. Yet, after the Democrats took over the legislature in the fall elections, every one of them was acquitted. My father called this "a travesty of justice" and was outraged. To add to his misery, General Butler was elected to the U.S. Congress in the upcoming election. Governor Chamberlain would never be able to attract Democrats and Republican supporters after this incident. In the fall, the Democrats nominated Wade Hampton as their candidate for governor.

Daddy won his bid for re-election, but Chamberlain lost the governorship to Wade Hampton. This election and the seating of a white Democratic majority in the state legislature signaled the end of Reconstruction in South Carolina. My father told us that Reconstruction ended in the other ten southern states at about the same time. He believed this was due to the simultaneous election of Democratic governors and Democratic majorities in their state legislatures.

"What did the Reconstruction government achieve?" I asked him, confused and indignant.

"Women took part in this political revolution, and that's a great step for the future," he told me.

"But women couldn't vote or hold office during Reconstruction," I stated.

He smiled his compassionate smile. "Lizzie, your friends and teachers, Charlotte Forten and Laura Towne, accomplished so much during the movement, even without voting."

I returned his smile. "Yes, Daddy, you are correct. They taught me a lot about the crusade."

"That reminds me of a question I was asked at a rally." He arched his bushy eyebrows. "A young woman asked me what wives should do if their husbands planned to vote for Democrats."

"And what did you tell her?"

He grinned mischievously. "I told her they should tell their men that they'd have to find another bed to sleep in."

My Daddy had a great sense of humor.

TWENT-TWO

Robert

The train was late. The Baltimore and Potomac Railroad was known for its lack of punctuality. But this was even more galling since I was eagerly waiting for Lizzie's train. She had been away at her New England school for so many months.

The train finally pulled into the railway station at 6th and B Street NW. She spotted me from a distance and started running toward me. "Daddy, I'm so glad to see you! It's been too long!" Her smile said it all.

As we embraced each other, I told her that this wouldn't happen again. "I miss you too much when you are away."

We laughed and interrupted each other's sentences while her luggage was retrieved. I finally hailed a carriage to take us to my apartment on 2nd Street. I was very excited to have Lizzie here in Washington to work as my personal secretary. She's so intelligent, and I knew she would do a wonderful job. I've been cheerfully enthusiastic just knowing she would soon be with me, and now she's here!

As a member of Congress, there was a great deal of correspondence to be read and answered. Having Lizzie close, both at work and at home, gives me something to look forward to every day.

A few nights after her arrival, I suggested that we have dinner at the Old Elizabeth Grill. I consider it the premier restaurant in town, and there's always the possibility of seeing a celebrity or two. I was eager to introduce her to my favorite place.

Thomas, my favorite waiter and friend, stepped out to greet us.

"Good evening, Congressman Smalls. Here you are with your lovely Elizabeth," he grinned, welcoming her with a broad smile. "Your father has been waiting for you with such enthusiasm."

My Lizzie reached for his hand and held it for a moment. "I'm so happy to be here, Thomas," she answered, beaming.

"And your father has spoken of nothing else for days," he replied, sending Daddy a wink.

I turned to her. "Allow me to suggest some of my favorite dishes, Lizzie. Thomas will guide us on the details, as always."

While we were enjoying our baked oyster appetizers, Thomas came over to inform Daddy that President Grant was coming through the door with Senator Hiram Revels. As they approached our table, they stopped to greet me and I introduced them to Lizzie. Both men were gracious and seemed pleased to see us and meet my daughter.

After they were led to their private table in the back, Lizzie exclaimed with glowing eyes, "Oh Daddy. The President knows you!"

I laughed cheerfully. "We all know each other here in Washington, Lizzie. If you work in politics, it's a very small town."

I leaned toward her and continued in a quiet voice. "Senator Revels has a very interesting political story. He was born a free man in North Carolina., fought in the Civil War, and served as a chaplain. Like myself and others, he has founded schools for the black children. He was also imprisoned in Missouri for preaching the gospel to Negroes."

Lizzie, eyes wide and questioning, gave me her rapt attention. She loved stories, especially about people she was interested in.

'Then what? How did he become a Senator?"

I laughed at her enthusiasm. "I could tell you the rest of his story, but why don't I arrange for us to have lunch with him soon and he can tell you himself?"

She clapped her hands. "Oh yes, Daddy. I would love that." Her curiosity and excitement were delightful. I sighed, wishing Hannah could have been here with us for that luncheon.

Lizzie quickly settled into my apartment and added the feminine touch it needed. She also cooked some delicious meals, and surprised me with her epicurean skills. She gave the credit to her mother.

"Did she teach you Italian cooking as well?" I challenged her playfully.

"Oh no, Daddy. Renata and her mother taught me that dish," she grinned. "I'll teach it to Mama and Sarah the next time I go home."

I could see that Lizzie was feeling comfortable with her new job and our lives together in Washington. We developed our working schedules and kept up with them. Lizzie and I arrived at my Congressional office at around 9:30 a.m., Monday through Friday. She read through my correspondence, answered my mail and kept the shelves and drawers tidy and organized. Then she went out to buy our simple lunch so we could work together another couple of hours after lunch. Because she handled most of my correspondence, I had the free time to do my work.

Lizzie was a quick learner and usually had her work finished by 3 p.m. I encouraged her to explore the city, knowing how much she loved being a tourist/student in Washington, D.C. As time went by, she met other young women and men, often joining them in afternoon tours or events. I was pleased she was learning about the city and enjoying herself. How refreshing to observe Washington through the eyes of my first-born.

───

Two weeks after she arrived, I made a luncheon date with Senator Revels in a small, quiet restaurant away from the noise. He asked his secretary to join us so Lizzie could meet another young woman who worked in the political arena. This turned out to be a great success, and new friendships were cemented that afternoon.

In the beginning, Lizzie seemed a little reserved, but Senator Revels quickly made us feel comfortable and relaxed.

I suggested he tell us about his background. He spoke about his religious affiliations and told us about founding several schools for the black children. He liked talking about his recruiting of two black Union regiments during the times he lived and voted in Ohio.

Lizzie glanced over at me. "My father also founded schools for the black children and recruited regiments. You two seem to have a lot in common."

"I respect and enjoy your father for many reasons," Revels agreed with a warm smile.

"I was elected by the Mississippi legislature to the U.S. Senate after offering an opening prayer in the state legislature. Fortunately, my words resonated with many," he laughed. Lizzie nodded, fascinated.

Lizzie interrupted confidently. "Senator, do you remember that vote count?"

Senator Revels chuckled. "Yes, I do. It was 81-15, and the vote was actually to complete the term of one of two vacant seats in the Senate."

Both Lizzie and Anita, Senator Revel's secretary, exchanged looks, appearing to be captivated with his story.

I interjected at this point. "Ladies, there's much more to this story. This was an historic event, and much debate occurred before this seating was accepted. For two days, the Senate galleries were packed with spectators. The Southern Democrats in office fiercely opposed seating our friend."

"But why?" asked Lizzie, stunned.

"It was based on the 1857 *Dred Scott* decision by the U.S Supreme Court." I said no more, allowing my friend to speak.

He picked up where I left off. "The U.S. Supreme Court had ruled that people of African American ancestry were not citizens. They argued that no black man was a citizen before the 14th Amendment was ratified in 1868, so I could not satisfy the requirement of the Senate for nine years' prior citizenship."

There was silence around the table. Finally, Lizzie turned to me and spoke up. "Daddy mentioned to me that you, Senator, had been a citizen when you voted in Ohio. You must have met the nine-year requirement before the *Dred Scott* decision changed the rules and decided that blacks could not be citizens."

I added, "And I was under the belief that the Civil War and the Reconstruction Amendments had overturned *Dred Scott*. The subordination of the black race was no longer part of the American constitutional regime. So, wouldn't it be unconstitutional to bar you on the basis of the pre-Civil War Constitution's citizenship rule?"

Senator Revels nodded, and added another point we were not aware of. "I was born an 'octoroon'—a mixture of European ancestry and African. No one had considered that, and I grew weary of fighting it. If they didn't want me, I was ready to step aside."

Again, silence prevailed. I decided to bring the conversation back to a positive light.

"Fortunately, on February 25, 1870, it was decided that your skin color could not bar you from Senate service. You were elected on a party-line vote of 48 to 8, with Republicans voting in favor and Democrats voting against."

Senator Revels laughed easily. "And everyone in the gallery stood up to welcome me in."

Lizzie beamed. "And after your term expired, where did you go?"

Senator Revels paused in thought. "I worked persistently for equality during my term, and then I was offered the position of president of Alcorn Agricultural & Mechanical College—a historically black college in Mississippi. Presently, I am teaching philosophy there, and I will soon take a leave of absence to assist the Mississippi Secretary of State in a detail where he's requested my skills, so to speak."

"Our friend is indeed a busy and sought-after man," I added. "And he's too humble to tell you he was the first black to be seated in the U.S. Senate, even though his time was limited due to uncontrollable factors."

We all enjoyed the lunch together, and it was obvious Lizzie and Anita would become friends. I was happy she was now learning new life styles, adding to the range of skills she already held. How quickly she had brought joy back into my life.

TWENTY-THREE

Elizabeth

My best friend Renata is coming to visit me, and I've made so many plans for us! Daddy is giving me eight days of vacation from work, and I hope to show her as much of Washington, D.C. as I can. It's been about four months since we've seen each other, and I have really missed her. She just celebrated her nineteenth birthday yesterday.

I made a list of what we wanted to see, including the circus. P.T. Barnum's *Greatest Show on Earth* will be in town, and both Renata and I are thrilled! I visited the theaters in the city and chose the opera performing at the National Theater—*Fidelio*. This is the only opera ever written by Beethoven. Happily, there will be a performance during her stay with us, and I have purchased tickets for us and Daddy. We studied Beethoven at the *Allen School,* and Renata wrote a paper on him for school credit. This performance at the theater will be her birthday surprise.

Renate arrived safely, and we've been spending our days visiting museums, parks, monuments, etc. We've also shopped for clothes and gifts, and we're both learning that the diversity in this city is incredible. I surprised Renata with an indigo-colored floor-length silk Japanese dressing robe, and she declared it to be the "nicest robe" she has ever seen.

"Happy Birthday, Renata! I'm trying to catch up with you in years and in style," I giggled. She seems so much more mature than I, and I have so much to learn from her.

Daddy joined us when he could, but was happy to give me the free time to show my best friend what makes Washington City so wonderful. He was eager to introduce her to his good friend, Frederick Douglass, and they got along well. I told her that Mr. Douglass was the only Negro who matched Daddy's celebrity in the political arena.

One evening, Daddy, Renata and I were dining at the Willard Hotel—my favorite restaurant and hotel—when a beautiful lady stopped at our table to greet us. Daddy invited her to sit with us, but she explained she was with another group. She said she'd join us for dessert.

"That woman, Charlotte Scott, is a well-known female Negro rights advocate," explained Daddy. "Our friend, Frederick Douglass, and I have spoken with her several times at abolition rallies. I think you would both find it fascinating to get to know her."

Fortunately, Charlotte Scott returned later and joined us for a pleasant hour of conversation. Renata and I liked her and enjoyed her fascinating stories.

"Do you ladies know the story of Antonia Ford, the woman who married the owner of this hotel?" she asked us.

"Wasn't she a spy during the Civil War?" I remembered reading her story inside the hotel's parlor.

Miss Scott's eyes twinkled with pleasure. "Yes, she was a Rebel who spied for the south by pretending to be from the north. She was captured and imprisoned. Her captor was Joseph Willard, and during her prison sentence in this city, they fell in love."

Daddy turned to Miss Scott. "Did she disguise herself as a man?"

Miss Scott nodded. "Among other things. She rode through the nights on horseback to deliver messages. This brave white woman used her beauty and charm for her cause. She reached the rank of major."

Renata grinned. "What a forbidden love they shared! And filled with danger!"

I added, "So she joined one side in the war while stealthily serving the other, right?"

"Indeed she did. In the parlor, you can see the photos depicting her life story. Both she and Joseph were handsome people, yet Antonia didn't believe he would wait for her sentence to be served and then marry her. She also didn't know he was rich and owned this hotel." I smiled. Miss Scott had opened another door for me.

Daddy later gave me a sweet compliment. "Lizzie, I felt so proud watching my young daughter conversing as an intellectual equal to the noted feminist. If only I could remember all the details to share with your mother."

Two days later, Renata and I spent the afternoon learning more about Miss Antonia Ford and her love for Joseph. We were saddened to learn they were only able to enjoy seven years of marriage. She died from complications of childbirth, in 1871, at thirty-two years of age.

"It appears that Joseph has not re-married. This is truly a beautiful story."

"Renata, are you seeing someone special?" I blurted out as we examined Antonia's photos. We had never talked about any love interests.

Turning to me, she appeared startled. "Not right now, but I was a few months ago." After a slow pause, she added, "It didn't last."

She never asked me if I had a special relationship with any man. Knowing me as she did, she knew I would have told her. But truthfully, I had never been interested in anyone yet. Still, I hoped she might have some romantic tales to share with me.

We turned to leave the parlor. "Look at her obituary, Renata," I whispered. It reads: *Whatever she thought to be right, she considered no sacrifice too great to accomplish it.*"

⁓

Daddy was happy to accompany us to the circus, which we all enjoyed tremendously. Seeing the non-indigenous wild animals was definitely the highlight for me. Renata was most impressed by a pair of Siamese twins. Daddy's favorite performance was effected by a small man (midget) who worked as an acrobat. We held our breath watching him walk on the tightrope high above the crowd.

"I've never seen anything like this circus!" exclaimed my father, grinning widely.

We all agreed. "I'd love to return next year," he said.

"You two are showing me a new world," laughed Renata. "Wait 'til I describe this to my friends and family!"

The ten days flew by, and after Renata returned to New York, I felt a deep sadness. It dawned on me that from here on, we would need to visit each other often to keep our friendship as close as it was now. My new friends in the area helped keep me occupied, but I missed the familiarity I have with Renata.

Daddy must have sensed the onset of my loneliness at her departure, because that weekend he said he had a surprise for me.

"Are we going away?" I asked him, hoping we were.

"Yes we are, my dear child. We're going on a train ride to Baltimore."

"Why?" I was not particularly fond of surprises, and wanted to know right away.

He gently lifted my chin with his fingers and looked me in the eyes. "It's a surprise. Just go pack and get ready. We'll be gone over the weekend."

We arrived at the Camden Street Station on West Fayette Street and my father hailed a carriage to take us to a small hotel near the Ford Theatre. The theatre owner was John Ford, the same man who owned the Ford Theatre in Washington, where President Lincoln was shot.

"Daddy, will my surprise happen tomorrow?" I wondered. It was rather late and I was thinking about dinner.

"Not exactly, Lizzie. Let's freshen up and go to dinner, and I'll tell you all about it," he beamed, happy he'd been able to keep his plan a secret from me.

What a grand surprise Daddy had thought up! He took me to the Tony Pastor Vaudeville Show, which was in town that weekend. Later, I found out it was the most famous vaudeville show in the land.

Vaudeville is a comedy without psychological or moral intentions, simply based on a hilarious situation. It could be a dramatic composition or light poetry, interspersed with songs or ballets. It was a very new concept for our country, and included popular and classical magicians, ventriloquists, acrobats, clowns, dancers, musicians, trained animals, jugglers and one-act plays.

This was the first time the two of us had shared such an unusual presentation, and I hugged Daddy and expressed my delight throughout the performance.

Both of us were surprised and thrilled at the variety of acts performed at this show. There were ten individual unrelated acts. We lost sense of time and place as we relished each one.

"Daddy, this was the most fun I've had in years! I only wish Mama and Sarah could have been here to see it!" I was very emotional and delighted with the show.

⁓

Renata's visit made me miss my home and my family, and especially my mother. I wanted to share all of this with her and Sarah, and when I told Daddy, he suggested that we invite them here to spend some time with us. They came to Washington the following month, and after their visit, we all traveled home together for the Christmas season.

Daddy and I jumped enthusiastically into the early holiday season in Washington D.C., filling our days with work and fun activities. Suddenly, Christmas was just around the bend. I think it was probably one of the most loving Christmases I've ever spent, because my grandmother Lydia, my half-sisters and their children, and all the other relatives spent this time with us. I knew I was growing up, and would soon be living life away from my family. And I also knew that obligations came with maturity. This would become clear to me very soon.

TWENTY-FOUR

Robert and Lydia

I was always happy when Frederick Douglass stopped by my office to drop off materials, newspaper articles, or just to have a conversation. Every meeting with him was enlightening. I was pleased that he'd recently decided to move to Washington, D.C. When we met together these days, we often discussed the upcoming election of mid-1876.

"My friend, I'm hearing a great deal about your recent involvement to get more rights for women and increase employment positions for Negroes here in the United States."

Frederick nodded. "Yes, I'm working hard opposing the 'Back to Africa Movement,' just as you are. I find it hard to believe there is still an interest in sending our black people to other places."

Frowning, I agreed "When I first started reading your articles, I saw that your motto was Right is of no set; truth is of no color; and God is the father of us all. If my memory is correct, that was back in the days of the *North Star*, your first abolitionist newspaper."

He grinned broadly. "And you memorized that, I see."

I nodded. "You must remember, Frederick. I was just learning to read in those days, and was educated by reading your writings, books, newspapers and speeches."

We were both silent, our thoughts flitting back to those days.

Looking over at me, he spoke slowly. "I often think about how much we have in common, even though we're from different generations. When were you born, Robert?"

"In 1839, almost twenty years after you. Something else we have in common is that we were uneducated as slaves, but we fought hard to get our education. You were self-taught; I was tutored as an adult, but we did it, my friend." Frederick eased forward in his chair and gave me a brief hug. Those moments meant so much.

After he left, I walked over to my shelf of favorite books and articles. After a few minutes of searching, I found a copy of the speech he'd given in 1852, entitled: *"What to the Slave is the Fourth of July?"* Frederick gave this speech on the Fifth of July of 1852, in Rochester, New York, and insisted that July 5, 1852 be the publication date. I re-read it and not only agreed with him, but applauded his wisdom. It started with a controversial beginning, but after hearing or reading it in its entirety, it was easy to understand what he was saying.

The speech was delivered to a local antislavery women's group. Here is the first paragraph. *America's birthday should be cause for both celebration and introspection. Some messages are designed to divide because we don't take the time to understand the full context. There will probably be many examples of this over the next few months.*

I read through it deliberately, and appreciated why many historians consider this work to be Douglass's finest oration. Arguably, it is one of the most powerful American political speeches ever written.

The first lines of the speech criticize the America of 1852 for not reaching the ideals of her founding documents. Douglass expresses his disappointment in America. Yet, he pivots further on, and states there is nothing in the founding documents that supports slavery. Near the end, he voices his belief that America will evolve toward meeting her ideals as society progresses toward a more enlightened future.

I suddenly grasped that in this regard, the words of Douglass are visionary.

Remembering our discussion about the election, I believe his words were prophetic. The disputed election brought us back together. Neither the Democrat Samuel Tilden nor the Republican Rutherford B. Hayes had the necessary electoral votes. However, there were a few states with disputed votes yet to be counted. Frederick and I shared some "what if" moments on this. As 1876 came to a close, the election still had not been decided. I knew that the American republic would still survive and progress, no matter what the outcome was.

I've mentioned the wonderful Christmas our family shared last year, and I asked my mother Lydia to talk and write about it in her own voice. She agreed to talk, but wanted me to be her "scribe," and I'm happy to give my mama anything she wishes.

I noticed a slight change in her that Christmas. For the first time ever, she looked almost feeble. She also seemed more tired than I'd ever seen her. Of course, I knew she was in her seventies and had lived a hard life. All I could think of was that now she deserved a peaceful period of rest and enjoyment of her home and grandchildren. I asked Hannah if she'd been sick, and she raised her eyebrows in surprise at my question.

"Robert dear, I would have told you if she had taken sick. She's the same strong, sweet Lydia as you've always known her. I believe your mother will out-live us all."

Then I asked Lydia the same questions. Here's what she wanted me to write.

Oh Lordy, I don't know why my boy is always worried about my health. There's nothing wrong with my body, except it's old. My concerns are few since my son and Hannah make sure I have everything I need or want. And right now, my ole' heart is soaring with the eagles, 'cuz my baby Lizzie is back at home.

That sweet grandbaby carries my name as her middle name, and that's the first joy she gave me that day she was born. From those days on, she's constantly filling my heart with happiness. I was so blessed to live around her for many years. Oh yes, I love my grandbaby Sarah too, but Lizzie is our first-born, and I've been her gramma longer. Oh, the memories of watching her grow up are so precious.

Yes, my body hurts, but it don't help by telling folks that. They jes' worry. I see it in their eyes. Now Lizzie is working for her Daddy and she's so smart. They seem so happy living together. I guess that's what they know and it works for them. I lived all those years without a husband, and I felt fine. Course Robert came along and during his younger years, I felt a great responsibility to teach him how hard his world could be. For a mother raising a child alone, you forever have to decide what's best for your child. Sometimes I wanted to leave him alone on his decisions, but he usually asked me for my opinion. Oh Lord, you gave me a good one in that boy.

And when Robert brought me dear Hannah to meet, I knew that very first night that she was for him. I felt in my bones that she would never let me or him down, thank you Jesus. And then, not too long ago, I started wondering about when Lizzie would find herself a good man, even though she's jes' finished her education. But I do want to be here when she finds him, and I want to be part of that glorious wedding. So, I take care of myself, eat and sleep good, and keep moving. Maybe I'll be one of those ancient ladies who jes' sit and rock away in those big chairs. And keep telling the same stories again and again. Hah!

Hannah brought me a fancy doctor who says I have rheumatoid arthritis. He asks if my joints hurt and how often. I guess he means "bones." Sometimes they swell up and I rest a bit; sometimes I jes' keep going. Hannah and I boil willow bark and some herb leaves that he recommends, and we make tea that helps me feel better. I have good days and not so good days, but Hannah doesn't bother me about not restin' when I should. She's the best wife to my son and daughter to me. I have no complaints.

When Lizzie's here, I seem to feel better. We go to church and the market together, friends come by to see her, and we all sit and tell stories about the past and Washington, D.C., and the importance of Robert's work in Washington and here.

"Lizzie, when are you gonna find a nice man to marry?" I ask her, with a chuckle.

"Oh Gramma Lydia, I'm having such a nice life working and exploring Washington with Daddy and my girlfriends. I don't have time to share that with a man." I knew she was strong-willed, and was very proud of her.

"When the Lord brings him to you, you won't fight that now, right?" I liked to tease her, and she laughed and hugged me.

"I hope I will know that he's the one for me," she answered seriously.

My son Robert looked over and said, "You'll know. Your heart will tell you."

Mama stood up to embrace me. "Look how God sent me your Daddy, and kept nudging me until I realized He sent him to me."

"Oh Mama, I want someone just like my Daddy. I'm willing to wait for him until that man is ready for me."

That's what I am waiting for. I want to be there when this beautiful soul marries her beloved. Every night I pray for that, and I know He's listening. Maybe we still have some time. I tell my body to stay strong until that day comes.

TWENTY-FIVE

Robert

Both Lizzie and I enjoyed attending political meetings, especially if we knew our friend Frederick Douglass was speaking or participating. Sometimes, when friends from Beaufort or Charleston were in town, we organized these gatherings in small restaurants near our apartment. I clearly remember the evening in 1876, when Samuel Bampfield found me in a tavern.

Lizzie was sitting at a small table next to mine, discussing women's suffrage with several lawyers. She had invited two other women friends to this meeting. The men at my table were reviewing a newspaper article published that morning, and relishing a rollicking exchange of opinions. I looked up surprised to see a tall young man I recognized approaching my table.

"Pardon my interruption, Sir, but I wanted to say hello to Captain Smalls."

"Well, hello Samuel!" I stood up grinning broadly and reached out to embrace him. "It's so good to see you! What are you doing here?"

"Looking for you, and here you are!"

"How did you know where to find me?" I asked.

He laughed. "We have a common friend, Elias Guthrie, who gave me the names of three small restaurants you frequent. I got lucky on number two!"

I invited Samuel to join me and my companions, and introduced him.

"My friends, I'd like you to meet Samuel Bampfield, a Congressman from South Carolina. He succeeded me as a member of the General Assembly. Samuel, meet my comrades from Washington and Charleston."

After they introduced themselves, Samuel continued. "I now represent my new residence of Beaufort. I've had the pleasure of meeting many people who know Robert here in Washington," he told them.

"What brings you to Washington, D.C.?" My friend Harold asked him.

"I come several times a year to meet with constituents or U.S Congressmen. We have concerns that we take to them, and of course, I especially esteem Robert Smalls, when I can find him."

Just then Lizzie stood up to take leave of her friends. I called her over.

"My dear Lizzie, do you remember Samuel Bampfield? You met him in Beaufort during our recess in 1875. Samuel succeeded me in the General Assembly, when I won my U.S. Congressional seat. "

They smiled and shook hands. "Yes, Daddy, I do remember him. How have you been Samuel? How are your parents?"

I was pleased to see that he held out her chair when she sat down.

Our conversation turned to Charleston and Beaufort, and the advantages of having lived in these great cities. As Lizzie participated in the conversation between Samuel and me, I could sense their mutual attraction, and was surprised how often they laughed together. Taking advantage of this opportunity, I excused myself and returned to my friends. I thought it might be wise to give them their own space, so they could get to know each other better.

Lizzie later recounted that they talked about their colleges. "Isn't Lincoln University the first degree-granting historically black College in the U.S?" Lizzie remembered reading an article about it, and just learned that Samuel graduated from there in 1872.

"Yes, Lizzie. So few black Americans were literate after the Civil War. Did you know that only five percent of blacks could read in 1865?"

"Congratulations, Samuel!" Chuckling, she continued. "I was only seven then, but Daddy and Mama made sure I read early and I've always enjoyed the written word. But you have set yourself apart from 95% of our people!"

Samuel nodded modestly. "Now, please tell me about your college," he replied.

And she did.

At this point it was getting late, but I didn't want to interrupt them. I saw a sparkle in my daughter's eyes and a glow on her face that I hadn't seen in a long while.

I was eavesdropping on their conversation, but careful not to get caught. Perhaps even then I was considering a possible union between Lizzie and this young man.

"So, Samuel, you became a pioneer black lawyer in Charleston!" Lizzie beamed. "You read law under Judge Cage of Charleston, and even I know how important a judge he is."

Samuel smiled pleasantly. "As you know, lawyers are uniquely trained for public service, and when I passed the bar in 1872, conditions were ripe for black leadership in the new Reconstruction government. Your father was active in the Republican Party and drew me in. He actually took me under his wing, along with a few others."

Lizzie laughed. "Daddy's personality is very effective in bringing others to his beliefs."

Lizzie briefly looked over at me, and then continued with her questions. "Aren't you the man who succeeded him as a member of the General Assembly?"

I watched Samuel as he leaned toward her. "Yes, I am."

Looking back at Robert, Samuel spoke to us both, "Thank you Lizzie. Meeting you again has made this a special evening for me. Thank you, Robert, for being here tonight." Daddy grinned.

"Yes, Samuel. I feel the same way." Her smile was tender.

He walked her over to where I sat and told me, "Congressman, I was so happy to see and talk to both of you. It is late now, and I should retire. Would you allow me to see Elizabeth again?"

I smiled at them. "I would certainly approve of that, but it is Lizzie who should decide." I was pretty certain I knew what her answer would be.

"There is one more thing I wanted to talk about with you. I actually did come to Washington to try to meet with you privately and talk about the race riots in Charleston. I know you're aware of the rising hostility between the blacks and whites. I want your opinion on whether we should consider employing more federal troops if conditions continue to worsen."

I nodded. "Yes. Why don't we have lunch tomorrow?" I suggested. "Would you like to meet back here at about 2:00 p.m.?"

Samuel agreed. We said our goodbyes and Lizzie handed him a piece of paper.

Suddenly, my thoughts turned to my dear Hannah, and how we'd met so many years ago. Hannah had seemed more reluctant to start a friendship with me than my daughter Lizzie was with Samuel. But I certainly had so much less to offer her. Nevertheless, she took a chance on me and changed my life. She would be so pleased to see how graceful and poised our daughter has become at eighteen years of age. And as her father, I couldn't be prouder.

Spring was a busy time for everyone, especially those of us working in the capital. The nation gave the impression of being more settled now than during previous years, but there was still a great amount of work to be done. Lizzie was indispensable to me. I wondered how I would have survived without her.

I was troubled about my friend, Frederick Douglass. He was still regarded as one of the country's most distinguished black leaders, but he had become somewhat disillusioned in his attempts to obtain a high government position. However, he had been granted various diplomatic and political appointments in recognition of his service to the Republican Party.

I spoke with him just before he delivered a powerful speech in April. This speech was presented at the dedication ceremony of the first public memorial for Abraham Lincoln—a monument to his role as emancipator, paid for by the contributions of ex-slaves.

"Why are you so uneasy about this speech, Frederick?" I asked him, searching his face.

He looked away, then turned back to me. "I'm not sure, Robert. I am very concerned about the rollback of civil rights as the Reconstruction period is ending. I need to emphasize that in my talk in order to mobilize black action."

He paused for a long while, and I waited while he collected his thoughts. "Oh Robert, I must speak strongly enough to ignite in our white allies a greater commitment."

I watched him closely. I could feel his torment as I realized his eyes were tearing up. Out of respect for him, I remained silent.

Finally, he spoke. "And I feel I am at a loss for the words to meet that goal."

I nodded. "Frederick, your speeches are always powerful, because they come from your heart. And since this discourse will be given on the eleventh anniversary of President Lincoln's assassination, I know it will be even more compelling."

His eyes looked doubtful, but he found the right words to clarify. "And then, I remember how I eulogized Lincoln as 'emphatically the black man's president,' but that's not been completely true. After hearing more of his beliefs, I now believe he was 'predominantly the white man's president.' And I don't know how to justify that in my presentation."

We sat silently while he battled with his conflicting emotions. I saw him scribble some notes, read them and tear them up. I quietly walked out of the room.

The next day, he showed me his new speech. He had managed to put this depressing alteration into thoughtful context, but the juxtaposition painfully revealed his disappointment. He delivered that vital speech to an enthusiastic crowd, and was given a long standing ovation.

At the end of the ceremony, Frederick expressed his dissatisfaction with the composition of the statue. He wanted an additional memorial to black self-emancipation. I understood his point and supported his position.

TWENTY-SIX
Elizabeth and Robert

My new friend, Samuel, and I met last Saturday to have "lunch on the Mall." I asked him what I should bring to eat and he said we could choose our food from the many stalls in the Center Market. Surprisingly, he knew the history and some facts about the Mall's construction. The designer's name was Adolf Cluss, and Samuel even told me some facts about his life. I asked him how he knew so much about it.

"Last summer I spent some time visiting a college friend in Maryland, and we took the Baltimore and Potomac Railroad to Washington." Pointing out the train station just west of the Capitol, he said that on the day they arrived at Washington, D.C., they ate on the Mall.

So we enjoyed a German lunch of dark bread, bratwurst and sauerkraut on the lawn, and then wandered leisurely through the Mall. There were small groups of musicians playing classical music in a number of areas, encircled by their own admiring audiences. Samuel took my hand as we walked around them, and I was pleased.

I studied classical music at the *Allen School* and explained to Samuel why I preferred the romantic, complex style of Baroque music. I mentioned Bach and Purcell in the conversation, and named my favorite pieces of music by each of them.

"But have you heard the *Centennial March* by Richard Wagner?"

"No, I don't believe I have."

"Then we shall ask one of these small orchestras if they would play it for us. It was commissioned to be written for the one-hundredth birthday celebration of our country. Some say it is proof that 'classical' compositions are now becoming an international service, and have lent status to important national events."

After speaking to several musical groups, he found one that knew it and offered to play it for us. I felt goosebumps as I listened to their magnificent presentation.

I turned to Samuel and hugged him. "Thank you for sharing this composition with me."

He grinned, returning the hug. "I'm happy I was the one who did."

I suddenly felt timid. "I have a question for you. I've noticed that everyone here calls you Samuel. Does anybody call you Sam?"

He nodded and chuckled. "Yes, my family does." Pausing, he asked me, "Would you like to call me Sam?"

I said I would, and he looked pleased. From that moment on, he became Sam to me, and then, Sammy.

Changing the subject, I remembered a thought I'd had. "The next time you come here, I want to take you on the canal ride."

"That would be grand!" he smiled. "I've never done that."

When he returned a few weeks later, we took the canal ride. The C and O Canal was built alongside the Potomac River and began at the mouth of the Chesapeake Bay near Georgetown. This canal ended in Cumberland, Maryland.

I was so excited because I had done my research. Even before we arrived at Georgetown, I was able to give him the history.

"In the beginning, this was run by mules towing barges up and down the canal on bordering roads. These barges hauled one million tons of cargo in 1875, which was the canal's peak."

Sam was listening attentively, so I continued. "The hull was built in two halves and put together after the boat was delivered to Georgetown. Each boat was eighty feet long and twelve feet wide. But they had to figure out how to install the locks. There were originally seventy-four locks that allowed the boats to raise 605 feet in elevation between Georgetown and Cumberland. Can you even imagine?"

"What happened to the mules?"

"Well, after the *Tom Thumb* locomotive proved its mettle in 1830, everyone thought the future of the canal was doomed. However, it has continued operating, along with the railroad."

"That's an incredible story," Sam said. "I also looked into the history. Just this year they built the Incline Plane in order to combat early traffic issues during the heyday of the canal. It lowered boats directly into the Potomac River to avoid boat traffic in Georgetown and delays there."

Our excursion turned out to be a delightful daytrip. I felt we were starting to know and appreciate each other, and I definitely liked what I saw.

I sensed that both of us looked forward to spending time together. He had just given me some good news.

"I know you're here and I'm in South Carolina, but I've put my name in for the position of 'clerk of court' for Beaufort County. I think it would be advantageous to live in Beaufort now, closer to my family and yours."

I wasn't completely sure what my feelings were for him, or even what was happening to me. I knew spending time together was bringing me joy, but I was also afraid of these new emotions.

I decided to talk about this with Daddy, since Mama wasn't here.

"Daddy, you know how much I enjoy spending time with Sam. He makes me laugh so much and I realize he's very intelligent. I've never met another young man as stimulating as he is," I said, with a bashful grin.

"Lizzie, this is the only young man I've seen you interested in since you've moved here. Did you spend much time with other boys during your school days?"

I nodded. "But just as friends. Sam means more to me than just a friend, and told me I'm his 'special girl.' But I feel so young compared to him, and I don't know if I'm mature enough to even think about a future together."

My father shook his head. "Eleven years older is not too old for you. You are very mature for your eighteen years and you've done so much. That's what you need to understand."

He gave me his warm smile as he contemplated his thoughts. "Lizzie, I know your Mama would be able to help you sort out your feelings. Summer is almost here and I have less work during this time, so why don't you go home for a week or two?"

I was too surprised by his suggestion to speak. As I thought it through, I knew it was a wonderful idea.

"Thank you Daddy. We should let Mama and Sarah know and I'll make the travel arrangements. Are you sure you can do without me for a week or ten days?"

"I'm sure. Ten days it is then. And when you return, you can tell me everything."

I jumped up and hugged him. How fortunate I was to have such a kind and intelligent father.

~

I got my daughter Lizzie off on her journey home and was now trying to sort out new political problems that were about to raise their ugly heads. One of the reasons I wanted Lizzie to go home was because I'm being forced once again to deal with my political debacle of 1872. While I was a congressman, The Southern Bourbon Democrats used violence and election fraud to try to retain control of the state legislature. I was charged with accepting a $5,000 bribe to vote for a joint resolution appropriating a payment of $350,000 for the Republican Printing Company. This never happened, but they wanted me indicted so that my opponent in the 1876 would be guaranteed my seat.

Back in 1872, I spent three days in jail and was released pending appeal. But I knew I was being framed, which infuriated me. And worse, that evil fabrication humiliated me when I returned to Congress.

The word in my small political world was that George Tillman, my opponent for my 1876 Congressional seat, was pushing for my arrest and indictment. To protect Lizzie from this newest plan, I wanted to keep her away during some of this time. Her life was moving forward, she was happy and seemed to be experiencing love for the first time. I didn't want to interfere.

After she returned from Beaufort, I discussed the accusations, the current investigations, etc., with her to prepare her for the future. She knew I had appealed the case, which was bigoted and prejudicial. She also knew I was supposed to have been lawfully covered by congressional immunity. My attorney insisted the case be given to the federal courts. In the end, my mock conviction was overturned in an agreement where charges would also be dropped against white Democrats accused of election fraud. In 1876, I was defeated by Democrat George Tillman, and when I ran for that position again in 1878, I knew I would lose. This would happen in the future. Today, I prayed that our lives proceed as smoothly as possible.

TWENTY-SEVEN

Elizabeth

Daddy had given me a ten-day vacation to visit my family in Beaufort. In the last few weeks, I've realized that I really miss Mama, Gramma Lydia and especially my younger sister Sarah. She let me know that she really needed to see me, and I knew that her age had a lot to do with that. Twelve years old is such a transitional time, and without a sibling close by, it must be very hard for her.

Thank God for the railway service that sorted and distributed mail on the trains. Even though letters took a while to arrive, we could communicate. Mama was so happy when I wrote them that I would come for a visit, and Sarah said she was "thrilled."

My life in Washington, D.C. has been going very well and I was anxious to share it with them. Daddy had less work during the summer, so this was the best time for me to leave him.

It seemed that everyone in Beaufort knew I was returning for a visit, because so many people came over to see me. The evening after I arrived, Sarah and I decided to sneak away to be alone and talk.

"Sarah, can you and I go to one of your secret places that no one else knows about," I suggested.

She smiled and, holding my hand, led me down to the sea to a place I didn't even recognize. I smelled it before

I saw it: the fresh scent of the ocean breeze. The fog was coming in—wispy as a steam bath. Just then, I heard the small breakers along the shore.

"Oh, I'm so happy the tide is out," I cried out. "You can smell creation: the salt and the fish and mud, the oysters and all decaying things. I've truly missed this smell."

She creased her brow. "Lizzie, you've been away too long. But I like how you describe it," she giggled.

"Sarah, can you hear the peeping and creaking of the tree-dwelling creatures?" I asked. "And, oh my! Just look at the colors out there. The light is reflecting on the water and the salt grasses. When the water recedes a little more, the grasses seem taller and reveal a golden tinge over the water."

Sarah smiled broadly. She tucked her arm through mine and I noticed her eyes were shining.

"You know what Lizzie? I'm feeling a warm happy surge sliding through my body now that you're back home."

We sat together on the soft sand, lost in thought and enjoying the music of the splashing waves.

"How is your life, little sister? Are you still happy at school learning new things?"

Sarah nodded energetically. "Yes, I am. Just like you were. But I just wish I had a best friend like you have with Renata." She looked away gloomily.

"Hmm. Well, remember that I didn't have one at your age. I think life is just too overwhelming when you're twelve. Your body is changing and your moods change as well." I glanced over at her and my heart softened. "Do you want to talk about that?"

After a long moment, she nodded, snuggling back against my arm as the air grew slightly cooler.

The two of us talked about everything we wanted to discuss for several hours. Sometimes Sarah seemed to be swallowed up by her emotions, and I tried to help her navigate through them. I knew it was difficult being the only "child" at home, and I told her I was so sorry we could see each other just a few times a year. I also promised her that I would do my best to change that, and be a major part of her life, even though we lived apart. I was determined to make up for that, and this home visit would be a good place to start.

Then she asked me about my life, and I confided that I was seeing a wonderful man I enjoyed spending time with.

"Is he tall, dark and handsome, like in the romance books?" she wondered.

Laughing out loud, I said, "As a matter of fact, he is! Are you already reading romance books?"

She giggled and nodded. "Lizzie, are you in love with him?" she blurted out in her direct style.

I playfully punched her shoulder. "Silly Sarah. What do you know about loving a man? I don't know him well enough to make a decision about love, but I can tell you that I like him very much. I hope you can meet him and tell me what you think."

"But Mama and Daddy fell in love right after they met," she argued. "Why can't you?"

Sending her my big-sister smile, I answered calmly. "I think it took them a little more time than that, but our world is different now. Women are working and leading more independent lives than Mama did. And remember, they were slaves and Daddy wanted to marry her quickly so he could live with her and protect her."

"Well then, if you two marry you can come back here and live in Beaufort! Then I could see you much more often."

I kissed her cool cheek. "I really like that idea, Sarah, and I will think about it. I know Sam will love you when he meets you, because you are loveable and wise."

She took my hand again as we walked home. I gave silent thanks to the Lord for bringing me back to Beaufort, just at the moment I needed to be here.

―

My time with Mama and Gramma Lydia was happy and filled with joy. I thought my grandma looked smaller and thinner since the last time I saw her at Christmas, but she assured me she was just the same as she was then. That dear woman never wants anyone to worry about her.

"Lizzie, your sister tells me you found yourself a husband over there in Washington!"

I burst out laughing. "Is that what she said? It's quite an exaggeration from what I told her, but maybe her prophetic words and her wishes can make that happen."

Mama walked into the kitchen at that exact moment and wondered what we were giggling about.

"Well, since Sarah started the rumor, let's talk about it," I volunteered.

I told them how Sam and I met, and that Daddy seemed pleased that we were getting on so well. I said we had seen each other a few times when he was in Washington, have had dinner together, visited friends, and we've gone to the theater. They were surprised that Daddy knew Sam's father.

"I believe I know that family as well," Mama said. "Isn't his mother's name Judith?"

"Yes. And according to Sam, they have been prominent citizens in Charleston's society for decades."

Mama said she remembered some earlier talk about the family being an example for diversity in a southern town.

"Yes, that's what Sam told me. There was a lot of pressure put on his father, Joseph, to marry a white woman, since he was white and British. But he fell in love with a beautiful free mulatto woman: Judith Robinson. And they got married and had eleven children! Imagine that!"

Mama nodded. "And the youngest son is Samuel, correct? And I've heard that he's Judith's favorite child."

"Do you know her Mama? Are you friends?"

My mother smiled. "No, I don't know her. I met her once or twice, but she was older and traveled in different social circles. I do remember her as a beautiful woman and well-liked in Charleston."

"So Lizzie, when's the wedding?" My grandmother was just like my younger sister. She said exactly what was on her mind.

Hiding my laughter, I smiled broadly and said, "We're not ready to talk about marriage. I'm still getting to know him, and I'm only eighteen!"

"Y'all better hurry up. I'm gonna be an ole' woman with a tired mind and body before long, and I most definitely want to be there to celebrate my first grandchild's wedding."

Reaching out to hug her, I assured her that she would be. I told them I wanted to know for certain that we were meant for each other, and for both of us to be confident we loved each other. Our feelings were already strong and pure, but this was still so new to me.

"Mama, I care a lot about Sam, but how do I know if it's love?"

She took several moments to answer, and then she spoke softly, "God will let you know, my dearest. Maybe you need more time, or perhaps he does. But when God knows you are both ready, He'll tell you." She reached for my hands and held them in her warm grasp. I felt a mixture of emotions swirling inside me.

Mama placed her finger under my chin and gently raised my face. My eyes misted and I let out a shaky breath as I breathed in the intoxicating scent of the night-blooming jasmine.

"Oh Mama, it's so hard living away from you and my grandma and sister. I need your advice and your wisdom."

"Lizzie baby, come over here by the window," Mama urged. "Tell me, what color do you see in the sky?"

I looked up and gasped. "Oh Mama, It's the color of ripe peaches!"

Mama nodded. "Whenever you feel sad and lonely, remember this Beaufort sky. Think about us, and just know we're always thinking about you. That will keep us close to your heart."

Gramma Lydia nodded and said in her quiet steady voice, "Lizzie dear, always walk with dignity, with assured grace and respect for yourself and others. That way, you'll discover the right path to choose."

TWENTY-EIGHT

Hannah

The sunny day was aglow with splendor on Lizzie's wedding day, April 24, 1877. Our lovely Beaufort home and gardens were decorated in glowing spring colors. Flowers, shrubs, and bright plants filled every available space in the yard. The atmosphere was joyful and overflowing with energy and love. Our entire family was gathered together, and Elizabeth was thrilled that everyone shared in her special day.

Lydia Polite Smalls, Lizzie's grandmother, finally got her wish. She always said she would not miss this wedding, and as the "reigning matriarch," she took her title very seriously. At eighty-one years of age, she was somewhat frail. Nevertheless, she dressed herself in a long pale blue gown and greeted every guest with her kind words and generous smile. With the help of my family, I oversaw the planning and implementation. As Lizzie's mother, I have dreamed of this day since her birth.

Lizzie was calmer than I expected, probably because she had the comfort of planning and sharing the details with her best friend, Renata. Together they organized and scheduled the particulars of the wedding. That week Renata became another daughter to me and another sister to Sarah, who followed her everywhere. "I wish you lived with us, Renata. Then I could have two older sisters to love." Their boundless fits of laughter filled our house with merriment.

Sarah was delighted with every aspect of the preparation, and her performance as bridesmaid was as gracious as it could be. She was only thirteen-years-old, yet she displayed the grace and style of a young woman. She told me, "Lizzie taught me how to be a proper young lady."

As their mother, my heart was full when I saw how affectionate and loving they had become to each other. Together, Sarah and Lizzie designed Sarah's bridesmaid dress—a light pink floor-length gown, made of crepe and lace. She wanted the sleeves to fit just "off the shoulders," to give her an air of sophistication. Her long dark hair was swept up in a twist, held in place by a beaded French claw clip.

Both of my older daughters also participated in the service, wearing their best fancy dresses and displaying their cordial manners. Charlotte was thirty-five now and her sister Clara was thirty-nine, and both were very handsome women. What a proud mother I was of these four beautiful children and my five grandchildren. Three of the grandchildren participated in the ceremonies as well.

Other than the bride and groom, the day belonged to my husband, Robert Smalls. He was elegant and refined in his Prince Albert formal cutaway coat, striped pants, top hat, and high-buttoned patent-leather shoes. In his short speech, he told his guests that his titles—general, captain, congressman, and chairman—were all hard won. "But the greatest, most important title I hold today is that of the father of the bride."

Lizzie was a resplendent bride. Her silk dress was sewn in the newest fashion, called the "princess line." Rather than a horizontal waist seam, it was molded snuggly to the body by vertical seams and tucks. This created a figure-hugging silhouette with a bodice that extended over her hips. Her beautiful bridal veil and jewelry complemented the divine image. I have never seen a lovelier bride, and when Robert walked her from the house to the garden, I clearly gasped at her indescribable beauty.

Samuel was dashing in his frock coat, featuring a waist seam with a full skirt and hemlines above the knees. He wore the four-in-hand necktie, which was a silk cravat fastened with a stick-pin. And of course his elegant gold watch chain was strung across the waistcoat. He looked very handsome and happy. His eyes radiated his deep devotion to my daughter. When he walked up to her and lifted her hand to his lips, I felt a tear or two slipping down my cheeks.

In addition to our friends and family, we rejoiced to have Samuel's parents, siblings, nieces and nephews join us from Charleston and Hampton. Another prominent guest was scholarly Francis L. Cardozo, also from Charleston, who founded the Avery Normal Institute and was Samuel's mentor and my husband's colleague. He was serving his third term as state treasurer: the most powerful position in the state government. Richard T. Greener, the first black graduate of Harvard University, also attended the wedding. He now serves as the first black person on the faculty of the University of South Carolina's School of Law. Robert also knew him and was very happy to have him attend Lizzie's wedding.

Robert's physician, political ally and former ambassador to Haiti, Dr. Alonzo Crum, arrived with his charming wife Ellen Craft. Ellen was an interesting woman. As the daughter of William and Ellen Craft, she spoke of her parents' daring escape from slavery in Georgia in 1848 and their humanitarian/educational service after the war. These experiences rivaled Robert's. After they discovered this commonality, our two families became instant friends.

Robert's political colleagues who attended the wedding were in our group of close friends who had purchased homes near ours. Among them were Judge William J. Whipper, Samuel Green, and George Holmes.

The ceremony was not long but it was definitely out of the ordinary. Robert's mother Lydia carried the rings and blessed them along with our preacher Reverend French. That was such a tender moment, especially to Lizzie. Once they were pronounced "man and wife," our family circulated through the crowd to greet everyone.

I tried to speak to most of the guests, but because of my "mother of the bride stature," I needed to oversee everything. Fortunately, my older daughters and Renata were helping out where needed, which gave me a little more time to mix with the guests.

Samuel's family gathered around me, anxious to learn more about us. After answering their questions, I asked a few of my own. His mother Judith was as elegant as I remembered, and Joseph was sophisticated and debonair.

"Did Samuel study in black schools during his early years?" I asked.

His mother smiled and answered enthusiastically. "Yes. He went to the Saxton School and his teacher was your guest and friend, Francis Cardozo, who had previously spent eight years there as a student."

I smiled. "Robert told me he's now heading the American Missionary Association's educational mission for black students in Charleston. And he mentioned that he opened the Saxton School in 1865. What a dedicated person!"

One of my kitchen workers walked over to advise me that dinner was ready.

Robert called them to the table, where Lizzie and Samuel were honored with short but humorous speeches. Our wedding dinner had been prepared by our cooks, under the watchful eye of my mother-in-law, Miss Lydia.

We began with sea turtle soup, followed by an excellent catfish and oyster dish, which was served with mashed potatoes on china plates. The succulent pig roast was the following course. My husband had supervised the preparations and cooking of the roast, since this was his favorite dish. He wanted to carve the roasted pigs himself, but I suggested we leave that responsibility to the chefs. The meat was served in thin slices, alongside various vegetable dishes.

The salad marked the end of the heavy courses. Our dessert was the wedding cake, and it was a tiered design of heavy cream, chocolate, and vanilla ice cream. My lady friends from the church perfected it, which made it more meaningful to Lizzie, who knew them all.

Finally, strong coffee was served in small cups, with a little cream pitcher on the side. And naturally champagne was available throughout and after the dinner.

At some point Robert stood up and approached the podium. "It has been my pleasure and honor to have worked these past two years in Washington, D.C. with my daughter Elizabeth. I am sorry to lose her as my congressional secretary and hostess, but delighted to leave her in Beaufort, where she will be a loving wife and a home manager." He paused to wipe his eyes.

"Hannah and I want them close to us, to enjoy them as much as we can. And of course to dote on the beautiful grandchildren we hope we'll have in the future. So, our wedding present to them will be a handsome home on New Street, just two blocks away from us."

The applause was rowdy and shouts of "Hear, hear!" could be heard across the lawn. Both Robert and I were overcome with emotion. After a moment, he continued. "Their home will be ready in June, and in the meantime, they will be staying right here with us."

This unforeseen surprise had been kept a secret from Lizzie and Sam, so they were as shocked as the rest of the guests. Lizzie threw her arms around me and her father and cried with joy. Sam seemed taken aback, but grateful and pleased. I was the happiest of all, because once again my daughter was back home in Beaufort.

The wedding celebration carried on beyond midnight. After the last guest retired, we fell exhausted into bed. But Robert still had enough energy to give me a long, loving kiss.

"Baby, we have been blessed abundantly, and we must give thanks to the Lord," I whispered in return. I wondered if he was still awake.

TWENTY-NINE

Elizabeth

We were very happy to move into our "new home." Actually, it was not new. It was built in 1830, and consisted of two rooms over two rooms. Daddy added extensions to the rear and double porches in the front. Our address is 414 New Street, and we now live just two blocks from my family's home on Prince Street.

I just recently learned that my husband Sam had been Daddy's political protégé since 1874. Sam's political career continues to evolve. In 1876, he was elected to the first of many consecutive terms as Clerk of Court for Beaufort County. He is well regarded and greatly respected by those who know him. He's as faithful a Republican as Daddy. William Elliot Jr., the son of the attorney who ran against Daddy for Congress, wrote this about Sam:

> He was a remarkable Negro...He was well educated and I remember that during the time I was in Beaufort he took up the study of Spanish. Many circuit judges said he was one of the best clerks of court in the state. Furthermore, he had the manners of a gentleman.

During my husband's one term in the General Assembly, he joined forces with the Republican black majority, opposing the appointment of white Democrats to judicial positions. Governor David H. Chamberlain vigorously opposed them. When the black Republican Speaker of the

House recommended the re-appointment of one Democratic judge, Sam rose to express his opposition.

"I have nothing against the man you recommend, except that he's a Democrat. Everyone knows that the Republican Party is on the verge of a terrible crisis. The only thing that can save it from utter annihilation is an out-and-out Republican judiciary."

That evening he shared his sorrow with me. "Lizzie, this is so important to the black population. We find ourselves living in a constant battle and simply cannot go it alone."

I tried to comfort him. "Dearest Sam, my father and others will support your suggestions. You don't have to do this alone."

He shook his head. "Lizzie, I don't think you fully understand. The experience of Reconstruction has demonstrated that blacks cannot go it alone in politics."

I flung my arms around his waist, searching his eyes. "Sammy, it seems to me that you believe you're seeing the handwriting on the wall. Am I correct?"

He gave me a sorrowful smile. "I fear that the success and safety of the Negroes lies in conciliation, not in antagonism in their dealings with the whites on state issues."

His prophesy would be revealed and come to pass over the next ten years.

∽

I was delighted to take up the traditional role of the full-time wife, home manager, and soon-to-be mother. Sam and I were thrilled to learn we were expecting a baby early the following year.

In the meantime, we needed to return to Washington to pick up my personal effects from Daddy's apartment. After years of attending primary and secondary school, working in Washington D.C., and just recently planning our wedding with Mama, I hadn't given myself time or permission for a period of rest. My husband came up with a wonderful plan: our upcoming trip to Washington would become our "belated" honeymoon.

"Lizzie, I will take you to the elegant restaurants and theaters you've spoken so highly about. We'll be like tourists, and together we'll enjoy things we've never seen."

"Oh yes, my dear! And I still have so much I want to show you. I've never taken you to the Old Anglers Inn, which has the best seafood anywhere in the city. And since we both love shellfish and delicious fish selections, I feel certain you will truly enjoy the cuisine."

That lovely old inn on the Potomac didn't disappoint. Sam declared that the oyster platter he savored was better than any oyster dish he'd ever tasted. After that impressive meal, we attended the National Theatre (built in 1835) to see *Hamlet*. Two of the original actors from *Hamlet's* debut performance at this theatre returned to star in the presentation.

We learned a great deal about each other. I loved his sweet way of making me feel so special. He had a soft, quiet manner of guaranteeing that my needs were met. I loved the way he watched my movements with quiet approval, the way his hand strayed to me whenever I was near, as if the touch of his skin on mine was necessary to him. Everything he did was encouraging. I was less obvious in boosting his confidence, but intuitively understood what I could do to please him.

We spent the days happily strolling through the streets of the city, calling on friends of mine (and his), and catching up on the news. We visited Hooley's Opera House for orchestral venues, and purchased small historical keepsakes to show off in our home. It took some time to organize and gather what we wanted to take back to Beaufort. Yet, this time for ourselves provided us an unforgettable romantic honeymoon. Perhaps we will not return to Washington soon, but we've now stored these beautiful memories in our hearts.

I put my hand in Sam's and squeezed it as we walked. "Let's stop and purchase something for our little one, who will soon be joining us," I suggested.

Sam laughed and hugged me. "Oh yes, I love that idea. Should it be a little girl gift, or a little boy gift?" he giggled.

I pretended to give that some consideration. "Hmm, how do you feel about something that will be perfect for either?"

"Lizzie, you always seem to know the perfect answer." I responded by tipping my back my head and lifting my mouth to his.

Gramma Lydia told me she would live long enough to see me married. She kept her promise and reigned as the lovely matriarch of our wedding, even though she was sick with rheumatism. A few months later, once she knew I was bringing a child into the world, she announced that her days on earth were coming to an end.

I often sat with her, massaging her hands and shoulders and listening to her sweet voice, while trying to conceal my tears from her. We talked about beginnings and endings, love and responsibilities. Every day I thanked God for bringing me home in time to love and comfort her.

She didn't want our sorrow, although she accepted it as part of our impending loss. She offered us her sweet smile while reminding us about her good life, and how greatly she'd been blessed.

Daddy and Mama spent as much time with her as she allowed them. They thanked her for all she'd been and done for them, and how she'd raised them well in spite of her meager means.

"Mama, you gave me a strong self-concept and strong moral values. You taught me that we are Africans, and part of a large family that was captured into slavery and brought to the New World against their will." Daddy's eyes searched hers, and his fingers closed around hers. "You also taught me to love and trust in God, and then how to love others."

"And dear Lydia, you showed all of us your solid religious orientation and resilient moral values. And hopefully, we've passed that on to our children," Mama added.

I smiled, overcome with tears. "I have always honored your personal integrity, and realized how you instilled a strong set of instrumental life skills in your son and your grandchildren. I hope and pray Sam and I are as capable and persuasive with them as you've been with us."

Daddy was taking his mother's passing very hard. He seemed to sense that it was imminent, so he spent most of her waking hours with her. They spent that week praying and singing together.

Gramma Lydia rose up on her elbows and, with closed eyes, began to sing peacefully. Daddy tried to join her, but his voice cracked with emotion. Hearing her fragile voice, I approached her room. I found Daddy with his head on the table, cradled in both hands, as tears streamed down his face.

Abide with me, fast falls the even tide.
The darkness deepens, Lord, with me abide.

So I sang with her. I sang for Daddy, and for Gramma Lydia.

Hold Thou Thy cross before my closing eyes,
Shine through the gloom and point me to the skies.

She opened her eyes at the familiar voice, blinking as she focused and gradually realizing that the voice was mine. I walked to her side and held her hand in mine.

Daddy wiped away the tears. "Mama, you are the most beloved woman I know," he told her. "I wonder how you've been able to hold both life's gifts and griefs so lightly."

Her eyes shone and she slowly turned her head to look directly into Daddy's eyes. "He'd 'a been so proud of you, son," she whispered.

"Who, Mama?"

"Your daddy."

"Please Mama, tell me about him." But her eyes had closed.

In the slowly cooling air, the crickets began their chorus, welcoming the coming night.

∽

Per her request, we buried her on Lady's Island, near the praise house on the old Ashdale Plantation, where she was born. We buried her with her ancestor figures that she'd given Daddy as a child.

Daddy told us that we also buried his unanswered question.

"Just before she passed, she spoke to me about my father." There was something so raw in his expression. "She said he was proud of me, or would have been. I couldn't get her to explain."

Mama held him close. "Who was he, my love?" she asked softly.

Tears rolled down his cheeks. "I don't know; she never told me his name."

"Then you didn't need to know, Sugar. She wanted that to be buried with her body and soul. We must remember that all her actions came from kindness, warmth and forgiveness."

My grandma had always known how to choose.

THIRTY
Robert

Samuel continued to make his family proud. As active members of the Masonic Lodge, he and I worked together on civic projects for the communities of Beaufort and Charleston. One of those services was keeping clean family plots in the Mercy Cemetery. After we die, we know our children will continue this practice.

Samuel, like his mentor Francis L. Cardozo, and a small group of mulattoes in Charleston, was a steadfast Presbyterian, who constantly studied the scriptures and quickly became an Elder in the Presbyterian Church. We had no black Presbyterian Church in Beaufort when he and Lizzie married, so their family often attended the First African Baptist Church. It was common for the Smalls and the Bampfields to attend two services on Sunday.

It took a few more years for Samuel to organize and take the lead in establishing the Berean Presbyterian Church on Carteret Street in Beaufort. He found a half-dozen investors, mostly family members and close friends, who joined him in worship there in that predominantly- black congregation.

Hannah's daughter Charlotte and Charlotte's thirteen-year-old daughter Emily lived in our big house on Prince Street. She had married Larry Williams in 1870, and they had a daughter named Rebecca. Two years later, they had a second daughter they named Susan. These were our first grandchildren, and I was particularly fond of these little girls. And finally, in 1877, Charlotte gave birth to my first male grandchild, Willie White Williams.

Hannah's second daughter Clara and her husband, an English sea captain named Ryder, lived in a house I owned on Craven Street. Their first child, Sarah, was born in 1872, shortly after her cousin Susan's birth. Beulah was born in 1876.

And then, in 1877, Hannah and I, as well as the Bampfield family, joyfully celebrated the birth of our daughter Lizzie's child, Julia. This was the beginning of the second generation of Hannah's and my direct descendants. We were now the proud grandparents of seven!

Hannah and Lizzie bonded quickly with Julia, and I was so pleased they both took the time to nurture her with stories of our black history. We knew that strong families build strong communities, and that our faith played an enormous role in our survival and achievements. Our family assisted in the building of churches and schools. From the moment Samuel became a member of our family, I realized that we were blessed with another solid Christian man to continue our fight to live and love as we pleased, under God's will.

If there was a bright side to losing the election in 1880, it was that I could spend more time in Beaufort with my grandchildren. I made them little toys, read to them and taught them what I knew. Over time, Hannah and I watched them grow into sweet and clever children. God tells us there's a time and a reason for everything. Losing the election opened up new doors for me and my family.

Before we knew it, Julia had a little sister, Sarah, quickly followed by Maria, who we dubbed Yaddie. Thank you Lord! We've been blessed with three Bampfield granddaughters in five years! We watch with gratitude how our other grandchildren play with, and help care for, these little ones. What a precious time for us all to enjoy together.

⁓

As a grandfather, I feel I must relate a horrific tragedy that happened a few years later. Hannah's first daughter Charlotte and two of her daughters, Rebecca and Susan Williams, were killed in a fire that destroyed the home they had finally purchased. Charlotte's son, Willie Williams, saw the flames on his way home from school.

"My only thought was to run and tell my grandfather, Grandpa Robert, who I believed could do anything. So I ran to his house screaming for him, but he was away in Washington. I was so furious and shocked that he wasn't there to save my family."

I later realized that my nine-year-old grandson Willie fostered a hatred for me for letting him down, just when he needed me to save his mother and sisters. I tried speaking with him about it several times, but he closed his heart to my words. Hannah's well-prepared words about forgiveness were not acknowledged either. So we accepted that we had to let it rest. His grief was simply too deep. Fortunately, Charlotte's sister, Clara, took Willie into her home and raised him as her son. She supported them all with her employment as a laundress, and would only accept financial assistance from Hannah and me during the Christmas holidays.

Willie went on to become a blacksmith and metal worker in Beaufort. When he moved to Orangeburg at age nineteen, he worked as a master mechanic in a shop owned by a German native named Von Oshen. At the age of twenty-one, Willie married "Miss King," who gave him a daughter they called Willie Mae Williams. His wife died and the infant Willie Mae was raised by her maternal grandmother.

Willie married Daisy John Gaither, named for her father, and bought some land to build a three-room house. They had ten children together, including an adopted one, John Avon Williams. In spite of all the heartbreaks that family endured, these children were raised to believe in the strong fabric of family: responsibility, education, respect, and family cohesiveness.

I was told that Willie never forgave me. I have given this to the Lord and I finally have peace about it. I do know that he encouraged others to honor family and community.

⁓

I successfully contested the 1880 election results and regained the seat in 1882. In 1884, I was elected to fill a seat in another district. I was also nominated for the Senate but was defeated by Wade Hampton in December of 1884. During my time in Congress, I supported racially-integrated legislation

I had the opportunity to help dictate and write a pension for the widow of my former Major General, David Hunter. That gentleman had done so much for our country, and his widow deserved to be taken care of.

Eventually, the political conversations about sending African Americans to the Northern and Midwestern United States or to Liberia made a comeback. Many black leaders, like myself, thought this was just another form of segregation. We opposed it vocally and in the written form. We wrote letters, articles and used other manners of communication to advise South Carolina African Americans to refrain from migrating.

Finally, in 1889, I was offered the plum position I had craved for a long time. President Benjamin Harrison appointed me to the post of "Collector of Customs for the Port of Beaufort." My responsibilities were many, but primarily consisted in collecting the duties on imports and exports. I was also authorized to commission ships to be used for the Revenue Cutter Service. I worked reference cases related to the Cutter Service's records and read and transcribed letters linked to the creation of this military branch. Because of my background, I found this work fascinating. At the time I was appointed, this position was only open to men. Fortunately, that would be changed in the future.

As an avid reader of history, I truly enjoyed reading the letters sent to the Collector of the Customs at Boston, from both the Department of State and the Department of Treasury. The letters written by Alexander Hamilton, Secretary of Treasury, and Thomas Jefferson, Secretary of State, were my favorite. I read every letter I could find that they wrote.

I can't express how thrilling it was to read and transcribe these letters, knowing I was helping provide the ability to search materials written by these men during that formative time in our country.

I wrote to my friends in Washington: *When I leave this position of Collector of Customs, I will do so with credit to myself, my family and my race. The Customs House at Beaufort, while conducted by colored men, can be easily attached to the top or bottom, for whatever inspiration it may be to the race.*

THIRTY-ONE
Elizabeth

A welcome breeze shifted the warm air and cooled us. We sat on the porch to enjoy the late afternoon's light wind and each other's company. My best friend Renata was staying with us, along with her husband Daniel and Antonia, their three-month-old baby daughter. My three-year-old, Julia, and four-month-old, Sarah, were napping upstairs, and we were now enjoying an hour of relaxation and companionship.

Mama and Daddy had come by to join us. Renata and I were drinking sweetened iced-tea because we were nursing our babies. Daddy, Samuel and Daniel were sipping bourbon on the rocks, and Mama made herself a lemonade. We've been remembering and sharing stories about the past, primarily to enlighten Daniel, who hadn't met my parents until today.

A few years back, Renata and I made a promise to visit each other every year, but with my two babies and her very young daughter, we almost missed this year. Train travel made journeying from Charleston to New York possible. The last time I traveled with Julia alone, I took our nanny with us.

Daddy was laughing merrily. He relished being the center of attention, especially with this very humorous story I had begun narrating. I was giggling as I spoke and probably didn't get all the details correct. The story was true, but so far I hadn't convinced Renata and Daniel of that.

"Congressman, is your daughter telling us this was written up in a magazine? What was the name of the magazine?" Daniel was very respectful and polite around my father.

I chuckled. "I'm not going to tell you a fib, Daniel. Yes, it was, but unfortunately, we lost the only copy he had. Remember, this was written up in the mid 1860's, and we've all moved several times since then."

"Hannah, you have such a vivid memory," Daddy began, "that you probably remember the exact conversation as it was written."

Mama reached over for his hands and squeezed them. "Of course I do, Sugar. I even remember the title of the story: *The Seed of Human Greatness*. And the name of the magazine was *Leslie's Illustrated Magazine*."

"Mama, could you please start from the beginning? We may have missed a little when I tried to tell it."

Mama nodded and looked reflective. "Well now, there were two freedmen sitting on the dockside, right here in Beaufort, talking about the war and the local news. They were friends, and they both had heard about my husband and the incredible story of his escape.

Looking at Daddy and then at me, she grinned. "I should say, 'our escape.'"

Mama paused for only a moment.

"That Robert Smalls," declared the first freedman, "he be the greatest man of all times."

"Cain't be," his companion objected, shaking his head indignantly. "You be wrong. How 'bout Jesus Christ?"

Mama's eyes twinkled with merriment. "The first man was confounded, but only for a moment. Then his eyes smiled kindly. 'That's okay,' he replied. 'Robert Smalls, he be young yet, my friend. Jes' you wait.'"

The men laughed heartily, and Samuel slapped his leg in pleasure, even though he was quite familiar with this story. Daddy, who loved for us to tell it, bellowed with delight. As usual, I felt a sweet moment of pride for him. It didn't happen often that a simple personal story meant so much to him. Our guests appeared to be a little awestruck, especially Daniel.

Just then, a pinprick of fireflies flashed in the low-hanging branches of a live oak tree in our garden.

"Oh, just look over there! I think those are fireflies!" exclaimed Renata. Then she smiled and addressed Daddy. "Mr. Smalls, I've known you for a while now, through Lizzie's stories and speaking with you over the years, but I want you to know what an honor it is to consider you a friend."

My dear Daddy stood up and embraced her. He really was a simple, humble man.

The election of 1880 marked the end of the decisive decade of the 1870s, during which the Democrats paralyzed and then destroyed Republican power, influence, morale and organization. The 1880s would see a changed approach that would be to "rationalize, codify, and legalize Republican defeat and national retreat." And the worse part of it was that disfranchisement of blacks would change from *de facto* by force to *de jure* through inventive legislation.

My father's contesting of his election results took so much of his time for those twenty-one months between the 1880 election and the day of the vote on the matter in the House of Representatives. The issue was resolved between Daddy and Benjamin Tillman on July 19, 1882. The vote was 140 to 5, with 144 not voting—a result showing the close division in the House. Daddy appeared and qualified by taking the oath prescribed. He returned to Congress for his third term. The first session ended a few weeks later and he returned to Beaufort for the upcoming election of 1882.

In the meantime, business failures, unemployment, and tightening credit heightened class and racial tensions and generated demands for government retrenchment. Property owners in the South demanded that state budgets be cut and tax rates lowered. Southern penitentiaries were dismantled and convicts were leased to private contractors. Spending on public schools and the care of orphans, the sick, and the insane was sharply reduced. Budgets for schools for blacks were cut heavily.

Not only my father, but most of his political friends, found themselves dismayed and disappointed with new changes. They realized that these events had the potential of changing the political structure of the state, and particularly the black man's participation in it. But Daddy now had his congressional duties to perform. He knew the end of a session was usually full of activity, yet he felt he had too little information on issues to contribute anything to debate. His one recorded initiative was the introduction of a bill to authorize construction in Beaufort of a building to be used as a post office, customs house, and other government offices. He also supported an appropriation to build a coaling dock and a naval storehouse at Port Royal, in order to support naval vessels in the harbor.

The Republican State Convention convened in Columbia. My father was elected to the executive committee for the state at large. He did some campaigning before the convention, including in Summerville, for the critical activities. My husband Sam was the temporary chair, an important position because one jurisdiction sent competing dual delegations. The thirty-nine delegates ultimately seated were divided between my Daddy, Edmund Mackey and John Lee.

By the second day, the division of delegates was: Mackey fifteen, Lee fourteen and Robert Smalls ten. Unfortunately, many of the delegates switched candidates, and Mackey's nomination was confirmed twenty-seven to fifteen. A man named Samuel Green was elected as the Seventh District chair.

Mackey defeated Lee, who decided to run in opposition. Republicans did poorly nationwide, but on the local level in Beaufort County, Republicans were returned to office. My father, while not a congressman-elect, still had his seat from the old Fifth District in the Forty-seventh Congress. On December 3, 1882, Daddy proceeded to Washington to resume his duties. His committee appointments were militia and agriculture. His singular legislative achievement in this short session was an amendment to the sundry civil expenses appropriations bill that provided $5,000 for the Port Royal coaling station and naval storehouse.

March 3, 1883, was the last day of the Forty-seventh Congress, and my father headed back to Beaufort, once again without employment. His fortune was about to take a turn for the better, but not before a shocking personal tragedy hit our family.

THIRTY-TWO
Elizabeth

Renata had visited me in Beaufort a few times over the years, but I'd never taken her to the Penn School on St. Helena Island, where I attended elementary school. Sam and I visited it with my parents a while back, but I always enjoyed returning and sharing it with others. Now I was excited to take my best friend and her little family. We decided to make it an "all-day" outing.

We started out walking toward my much-beloved schoolhouse. We passed through small fields of palmettos divided by majestic live oak trees. Spanish moss dripped from every available limb. I pointed out the bright red fungus growing on the side of several trees. White mushrooms were sprouting up everywhere.

Even before we spotted the schoolhouse, I told them how we got it on the island.

"In 1865, the Philadelphia Freedmen's Relief Association sent down the first real schoolhouse by boat, and they erected it to face the Brick Church. They fitted it with a fine brass bell and named it Penn School, after the great defender of freedom, William Penn."

A slow smile spread across my face as we caught sight of the Brick Church in the distance.

"Look over there at the oldest building here," I pointed out. "It's the 1855 Brick Church, built by the plantation owners of the island. We used it for many meetings, educational programs and gatherings. My parents have supported it since I was about Julia's age."

"Can you give us the history of the island?" asked Daniel. He was a student of history and quickly pulled out a pen and notebook from his shoulder bag.

"Yes I can, at least some of it. The school was established during the Civil War, and it's the first school for freed slaves following emancipation. When the last of the Union troops left, 12,000 native and refugee freedmen stayed on the island, with about 40% white residents. For another half a century, there were about 50 whites to 6,000 Negroes."

Now Renata's curiosity was piqued. "But what about the original slaves? How did they get here?"

I turned and smiled at Sammy. "Darling, I know this is the part you love to talk about."

With an eager grin, he took over the narrative. "Yes, the school is an active educational institution and Lizzie and I also support it. The history of the first inhabitants is quite fascinating."

I knew that Sam's version would be accurate and well-told.

"The slaves were brought over to the island by the English in 1659, and were primarily from east Africa. In the later 17th century, the government made a provision that all ships trading with Madagascar had to deliver one slave to St. Helena. These slaves were not treated badly because of a 1673 order from London: *We order that all Negroes, both men and women living on said island, that shall make profession of the Christian faith and be baptized, shall within seven years after be free planters and enjoy the privileges of free planters both of land and cattle.*

Daniel was impressed. "Sam, did you memorize that order, or invent it?"

Sam's mischievous grin said it all. "I memorized it, because it pleases my wife that I am so interested in her school."

He continued. "In 1792, a new set of slave laws was written, saying that no new slaves could be imported to St. Helena. Fifteen years later, in 1807, the slave trade was banned throughout the British Empire. However, this didn't free the existing slaves."

"When did they free them?" Renata wondered.

"That happened on August 1, 1834. After that, any slave older than six years of age would be freed but still remain at work, becoming an apprentice laborer."

"So these slaves became free long before the slaves on the mainland and in other states, correct?" Renata seemed impressed.

I nodded. "But I learned at the Penn School that slaves still remained the property of their owners and could be bought and sold. So that leaves a lot to interpretation as to how well their owners chose to treat them."

"Lizzie, you were taught by the school's first black teacher, right? What's her name?"

I smiled, remembering how much I loved Miss Charlotte Forten.

"Her name is Charlotte Forten," I smiled. "Why don't we walk a bit and I'll show you some of my favorite places. This is truly a lovely island and I want you to see more. I know a quiet and shady place where we can eat the food we've prepared, and after we eat I can tell you more about how the school began."

Everyone agreed, so we continued our walk. The men talked about "men things" while Renata and I played with our babies. Mama had offered to spend the day with Julia, giving me more time for little Sarah and our friends.

We ate and relaxed on the beach in a shady area under a huge oak tree. Our babies nursed and slept, and Renata and I closed our eyes for a few moments while our husbands waded in the water. When they returned, Daniel sat with us and asked Sam and me several more questions about the island.

I began slowly, so he could write notes in his little book. "Public education began June 18, 1862 in small rooms where cotton had been stored. Miss Ellen Murray, a Quaker teacher who came down from Pittsburgh, Pennsylvania, and Laura Matilda Towne, an abolitionist missionary, brought the teaching materials and set up the room for their pupils. They gathered nine women, all ex-slaves, and taught them in a back room of the Oaks Plantation."

Sam sat down beside me and continued the story. "After a few weeks, there were forty-seven adult pupils, and soon they started bringing their children. In October, they asked for and received permission from General Saxton to use the Brick Church on the corner plantation. Miss Ellen Murray and Miss Laura Towne were now teaching one-hundred and ten pupils!"

I nodded. "Yes, and at a later time there were about forty little schools scattered around the island in the old cotton houses. Ellen Murray was teaching almost two hundred students in the Brick Church. And then Miss Towne came down here to help. She traveled the sandy roads with a doctor's bag in her buggy, because she had studied homeopathic medicine in Pennsylvania."

Sam added, "Other missionary teachers came down to help, but about a year later, most of the little school rooms had closed down. Missionary teachers were unable to cope with the climate and the fever seasons and returned to Pennsylvania. So most of the little schoolrooms closed. A few a few remained open and were taught by the older pupils of Miss Murray."

"When did the real schoolhouse arrive?" asked Renata.

Sam answered her. "In 1865, the Philadelphia Freedmen's Relief Association sent the first real schoolhouse down by boat."

"You two should write down this history and make it available to everyone," suggested Daniel.

I laughed. "Daniel, you can do that. It looks like you've done your research."

I knew they had enjoyed the day in St. Helena. But I still had one more thing to share with them. "Most inhabitants of St. Helena Island live out their lives on land handed down to them by family. They don't feel the burden of segregation that has embittered the lives of blacks elsewhere. The great simplicity and poverty of their lives has been somewhat balanced by the basic security of living on their own land."

Sam finished my thought. "They walk in dignity, with assured grace and respect for themselves and for others."

Renata reached for my hand. "What a lovely place, and the history behind it is special. Thank you, Lizzie. This day will never be forgotten."

I nodded in agreement. Walking slowly back to the dock, we could hear the crickets beginning their chorus, welcoming the coming night. The cicadas and hoot owls joined them, and several moments later, we looked over the horizon and saw the brilliant orange sun dipping into the edge of the water.

THIRTY-THREE

Elizabeth and Robert

I had convinced Daniel and Renata to stay with us long enough to visit Charleston. Renata and I have been there in the past, but never during the horse racing season. Daddy took Mama, Sarah and me on two different occasions to the thoroughbred races, which quickly became my favorite thing to do in that city.

The Washington Race Course was a one-mile loop around the middle of Charleston. It opened in February of 1792. Its main event was the Jockey Club Purse, a race of four heats. It was always held one week in February over four days: Wednesday, Thursday, Friday and Saturday. Tavern-keepers rented houses near the track to use as restaurants, bars and inns. The race itself was bursting with excitement and thrills. I think it was the most pleasurable single-day event I've ever attended.

But watching the races was only a small part of it. There was a wide variety of other amusements, such as a showplace and a sales arena. I saw eight thoroughbred horses, imported from England, sold through auction! Every moment there was thrilling!

Imagine my sorrow and frustration when I learned that, this year, the race in February was their final one. The grounds were now leased to a man for pastureland.

"That was the principal reason I planned a three-day visit for us," I told them unhappily.

"I'm sure there are many other places we can go," suggested Sam. "How about the Floral Fairs? I've never been and you and your mother really enjoyed them."

Renata added, "Oh yes, Lizzie. Perhaps we can return to the Charleston Theater, or attend the Dock Street Theater. You know how much we all love to eat, and that city has every type of cuisine we could ever desire."

They convinced me that one day the race track would be re-built and we would go to the races then. In the meantime, we made plans to attend the Floral Fair on the third of May. This was considered to be the first fair event ever held in the city of Charleston. Our tickets had to be purchased in advance, and we traveled round-trip on the railroad lines for the price of a one-way ticket.

We booked rooms at the *Planters Inn* on Meeting Street, since the Floral Fair was held in the Agricultural Hall just down the street. This beautiful inn was built in 1844, in a prime location on the corner of Market and Meeting Streets. The Agricultural Hall fit right into this historic area. There was a large flower tent measuring forty by sixty feet. It covered the numerous abundant and rare plants on display. After dark, we watched the lighting of the tent and main hall, provided for the very first time by electricity. This replaced the original gas lighting and provided such a bright environment.

The awards were announced around five o'clock, followed by a promenade concert by the Metz's Band. Ice cream and refreshments were offered. There were no cash awards for the winners of the twenty categories, but instead, they gave out valuable keepsake items. This included a silver napkin ring, a silver knife and a gold pen.

"You've done it again, Lizzie!" laughed Daniel. "What a unique venue and what beautiful flowers, plants and rare vegetables we've discovered. All we had to do was take it all in and enjoy."

We walked over the cobblestone streets, taking pleasure in the sights of the city. Renata and Daniel wanted to walk down by the Battery—the defensive seawall and promenade.

"Why do they call this area the Battery?" Daniel had his notebook ready for the answer.

"Because it's named after a pre-War coastal defense artillery battery," said Sam. "The British built it and named it."

We returned to the *Planter's Inn* and freshened up for the evening. After feeding our babies, we felt very comfortable leaving them with our nanny Berta, who was so happy to join us on this trip. I had planned a big surprise for our guests as far as the dinner house I chose.

"Darling, why won't you share this news with me?" Sam asked as we were dressing. He pretended to pout, but his eyes twinkled. He also enjoyed being surprised.

"Well, Sammy, then it wouldn't be a surprise, would it? I believe you will be very happy with the site I've chosen."

McCrady's Tavern overlooked the bay and had been the hub of social life in Charleston following the American Revolution. It was constructed in several phases during the second half of the 1700's. Then it was purchased in 1778 and expanded. I shared this history with them as we walked the short distance to the tavern.

"And, here's the part you historians will appreciate knowing. In 1791, the *Society of the Cincinnati* hosted a banquet for President George Washington in the Long Room, where we'll be dining this evening. He was visiting the city for several days."

Once we arrived, I basked in their spontaneous and favorable reactions.

"This place is remarkable," exclaimed Renata. "I've never seen such an authentic tavern from last century!"

Daniel grinned widely and stayed silent as he took it all in. "I feel like I'm living during the American Revolution!"

Sam placed one of his hands over mine as we were being seated. "My lady of surprises," he dubbed me. "Always finding the most unusual things."

The waiter smiled as he handed us the menus. "Most people find it interesting that this Long Room was used for theatrical performances and banquets for the city's elite. It is the last of its kind in Charleston."

We dined on several elegant dishes, including blue crab salad, Berkshire pork, duck fat roasted beef tenderloin, and broken arrow antelope, among other delicacies. And after that, we all shared a chocolate truffle cake. I was so happy with everyone's enthusiasm. I smiled, knowing we still had two more days to explore and enjoy.

While Lizzie was planning and appreciating the Charleston visit with Renata and Daniel, I was back in Washington. Upon my return to the city, I learned about the passing of my friend Frederick Douglass's wife, Anna Murray Douglass. I had met her on several occasions and admired her greatly for her work with the *Underground Railroad*.

One of my Washington acquaintances asked me what that term meant.

"Well, my friend, it wasn't underground nor was it a railroad. It was a network of people, both whites and free blacks, who worked together to help runaways from slaveholding states travel to states in the North and to Canada, where slavery was illegal.

"Do you know people who did this?" he wondered.

"Indeed I do, and most probably some of your family members were involved in one way or another."

Frederick agreed to meet with me in his home. I found him disheartened and dispirited, and I wanted to cheer him up.

"My Hannah and children, as well as I, send condolences to you and your children," I told him sincerely.

Watching his face, it seemed that several emotions were competing with each other, I felt briefly overwhelmed by his sadness.

"I am devastated without Anna. I'm trying to keep busy with my writing."

"What are you working on now, Frederick? Do you have another book in mind?"

He turned so that his face was inches from mine. "Not now, Robert. Lately I've been ruminating over the *Black Codes* and trying to see what we can do about rectifying them in some way."

"But my friend, they were repealed in 1866! When Reconstruction began," I answered cautiously.

"Supposedly. But look where we are today! Many of those Codes were re-enacted in the Jim Crow Laws.'"

I knew he was right. Even though a Civil Rights law, introduced by Senator Sumner and Benjamin Butler, guaranteed equal treatment of blacks and whites in all public places, this was not practiced in most southern states.

Looking up sadly, he rose to search his bookshelf. "Even the United States Supreme Court did not help our cause." He opened up one of his tomes and read: The Dred Scott decision was the U.S. Supreme Court's ruling on March 6, 1857, that having lived in a Free State and territory did not entitle an enslaved person, Dred Scott, to his freedom. In essence, as someone's property, Scott was not a citizen and could not sue in a federal court.

"And this Jim Crow drivel we're all discussing to block black voters cannot continue," I said angrily.

He nodded, his eyes downcast. "Smalls, we must do something to somehow convince the other blacks and whites to follow suit!"

I reached for his hand. "Frederick, you are the undisputed leader of the black people. They will listen to you."

We sat in silence a while longer, alone with our thoughts. I took his powerful words into account.

When I finally spoke, I kept my tone light. "What I'm concerned about is the law that blacks can hold local offices in local elections, but they are suppressed from voting in state and national elections."

Frederick stood up and looked steadily into my eyes. "Blacks cannot remain half-black and half-free! We must give them all or take all from them. Until this half-and-half condition is ended, there will be just grounds for complaint. Until the public schools shall cease to be caste schools in every part of our country, this discussion will go on."

Returning the tome to his library, Frederick walked to my chair. "With the end of Reconstruction and the Compromise of 1877, oppression of African Americans became rampant under the Jim Crow Laws. Hence, the quest for Civil Rights and the struggle for equality will continue. I do not believe you and I will see an end to it."

I stood up and gently enfolded him in my arms. "Take all the time you need, Frederick." I repeated supportive phrases while I rubbed his back.

"Let not your heart be troubled, dear friend," I told him. "God is in control, and His will shall be done."

His eyes misted. "Thank you for that, Captain Smalls. And thank you for coming by for a much-appreciated visit."

I left his home feeling encouraged that I had given him some comfort and perhaps, even a little hope.

THIRTY-FOUR

Robert

I've written so many letters, articles and papers over the years, and nothing has been harder to compose than this one. I am devastated and my heart is shattered. My darling Hannah is no longer with us. She passed away on July 28, 1883, and I didn't even realize the moment she left, lying next to me in our bed. A sudden heart attack took her during the night, leaving me stunned with shock and unbearable grief.

A few months ago, she mentioned a pain in her chest, and I told her to lie down until it passed. Another time she said she had a stomach ache, which we attributed to the large dinner we'd consumed with our children. Hannah had always been in great shape and good health. Over the years, we'd both put on a few extra pounds, but she remained strong and energetic. I started gaining weight, so she insisted we cut out some fat in our meals. And for a fifty-eight year-old woman, Hannah was active.

After conferring with several doctors, I was told she had died from coronary atherosclerosis, or angina pectoris. Her cause of death was from insufficient coronary circulation. We knew nothing about this, and were not prepared.

Every day I reflect on how much I love her and how she returned my love. I remember how I fell in love with her from the first day I met her. When I think about the incredible "escape" we shared with our two little children, tears roll down my cheeks. The pain is so intense I sometimes feel as though my heart will shut down.

I have nightmares that this dark empty loneliness will swallow me up and devour me. There are many nights I wish it would. Sometimes, in the middle of a conversation with friends or family members, tears suddenly sting my eyes, and I feel them overflowing and trickling down my cheeks. Other nights, I wake up sobbing. I wonder if it is possible to die of heartbreak.

I know I must think about my children and my grandchildren. They need me in their lives, especially the little ones, now that Hannah isn't here. I could never replace Hannah, but I can play with the children and tell them stories. I can encourage them and keep her memories alive for them.

Sarah and Lizzie are spending much more time with me and they both look exhausted. I needed to find something to take my mind away from my loss. Sarah came up with a solution.

"Daddy, I think you need to return to your political life. That's where you come alive with ideas, your proposed bills and the speeches you give. That's one way you can feel helpful to others, and will give you purpose again."

Lizzie nodded and smiled. "I agree, Daddy. And when you do, Sarah could become your secretary and social director, like I was."

I listened to them and forced my mind to at least consider this possibility. I could run for Congress again in 1884. But my energy level had shrunk to the point that my mind couldn't absorb those ideas.

Then, unexpectedly, my friend and mentor Frederick Douglass appeared at my door. He seemed even taller and his bushy white hair was even whiter. His first words to me were that "divine intervention" had sent him.

"My dear Frederick, I only received word this morning that you were coming. Thank you, Lord, for intervening!" After a warm embrace, I took his arm and guided him inside my home.

Our reunion brought me some happy moments, and also tears. Frederick was still in mourning for his wife, yet he came to console me. I never considered how important men's friendships could be. During emotionally difficult times, we need each other. He understood this and came as quickly as he could.

"Where did you bury Hannah?" he wondered.

"She's in the yard cemetery at the First Tabernacle Baptist Church. Would you like to visit her?"

Frederick smiled and nodded. "Yes, I would. Let's go there together. Is this a good time?"

The moments spent with him were soothing and therapeutic for me. He met Sarah and remembered Lizzie and Sam from previous encounters in Washington.

The two of us spent three days together, and Lizzie made certain he was well-fed and entertained. He met our grandchildren and spent time walking along the Battery with me. I introduced him to several of my old friends. I am eternally grateful that he came at just the "right time," because he convinced me to put in my name for another run for Congress.

"You need to wrap your head around the country's issues once more, Smalls. And God knows your state of South Carolina needs you there," he said.

"But I have little time to prepare for this," I objected.

"So make the best of it," he grinned. "And it will help you to bear the sorrow of Hannah's passing. Remember, my friend, I know of what I'm speaking."

My daughters and Sam agreed with Frederick's advice, and so I ran for office. Luckily for all of us, I won, defeating a white Democrat attorney and Confederate veteran, William Elliott.

"Oh Daddy, please take me with you," pleaded Sarah, after the results of the election were announced. "I'll learn quickly, and I can still finish school there."

We arrived in Washington and my twenty-one year-old daughter enrolled in the Minor Normal School to finish up her education. She also helped me in my office, and it was a personal gratification to live and share my apartment with her. Sometimes when I look at her, I see my Hannah. They definitely resembled each other, even in their personalities. I was beginning to feel my heart healing, and thanked God for my blessings.

I've been told I made one delightful short speech on the floor of Congress during my last period. I was arguing in favor of a bill I had introduced to provide a pension to General Hunter's widow, Maria. That man had done so much for me personally, including sending me to meet President Lincoln. General Hunter had recently passed into eternity, not too many months before Hannah.

The year was 1885. A portion of my short speech is below.

Mr. Speaker, by the variations and methods of modern politics, my race of upward seven millions of people is represented on this floor by myself. How long this injustice will be tolerated I will not dare to prophesy; but so long as one of us not be withheld from any measure of legislation which will add to the prosperity and happiness of all the people, without regard to color or condition, and the permanence and greatness of a common country, our work will continue.

The bill for General Hunter's widow ultimately failed, even though it passed both houses of Congress. Then it was vetoed by President Cleveland. I was appointed to the Committee on War Claims and sponsored a number of private relief bills. I appealed several decisions and offered several amendments that were not acted on.

I returned to Beaufort and campaigned on the state level against William Elliott in 1886. When the election was certified, it was Elliott over Smalls, 6,493 to 5,961. I challenged these results, but eventually gave up, after conferring with Frederick Douglass in Beaufort. He and I, along with former senator Blanche K. Bruce and former representative John Lynch, prepared a declaration calling for black support of Harrison's bid for the presidency.

At that point, I was persuaded to step aside in favor of a younger man for the Seventh District seat in Congress. Thomas Miller was ten years younger than I. We had to accept that the Republican Party had been destroyed as a political force. The South Carolina Democrats united behind Elliott for the seat in Congress, and many problems arose during that election period. The Fiftieth Congress adjourned, making way for the Republican-majority Fifty-first Congress to be seated in December, 1889, and for Benjamin Harrison's inauguration.

THIRTY-FIVE
Elizabeth

My father had been considered for the coveted position of Beaufort's Customs Collector since 1885, but it wasn't until President Benjamin Harrison decided to give him this appointment in 1889, that he finally received the commission. He held that office until 1913, except during President Grover Cleveland's second term. President William McKinley re-appointed him in 1898, and he served in that post until June 1913, when he was forced out by two white South Carolina senators who blocked his re-appointment by President William Howard Taft.

After Daddy's death, I found a short article he had written while still the Customs Collector. Perhaps he had a premonition of what awaited him. *During the twenty odd years I have held the position of collector, I have succeeded to manage affairs so that when I leave it, I will do so with credit to myself, my family, and my race...the Customs House at Beaufort, while conducted by colored men, can be easily attached to the top or bottom, for whatever inspiration it may be to the race."* He believed he was in the perfect position during those years of his life.

The first two years after my mother's death were very hard on Daddy. Watching him grieve the death of the love of his life, I wondered if he would ever be able to surpass this loss. I asked him.

"Lizzie, I've tried to overcome my grief, and it doesn't work. So now I'm asking God to teach me how to live with the love she left behind."

Sarah and I also mourned our mother's death, but in different ways. I knew I had to be the one to show restraint, so my Daddy and my sister had some guidance. I also suffered from her death and the great loss in our lives, yet I tried to hold close to my heart the happy memories and the many demonstrations of love she had given us.

Samuel and I continued to have children during these years. By 1889, when Daddy had finally become the Beaufort Customs Collector, I had birthed six children. Maria, Robbie and Lizzie joined Sarah and Julia. Our baby, Hannah, died in infancy—another sad loss to grieve. Our other children were blossoming, and Daddy played an important role in helping me raise them. They loved having their Grandpa around.

My husband, Samuel, was perpetually occupied with his various careers, but he also gave valuable time to our family. He worked as an attorney in Beaufort and Charleston, became the Clerk of Court in Beaufort for twenty-one years, and served in the South Carolina House of Representatives from 1874-1876. He tried to include Daddy in some areas of his work, which helped restore my father's self-esteem.

In 1891, Sam joined with G.W. Anderson, a schoolteacher, and Randall Reed, an attorney and deputy sheriff, to become the founding editors of the *New South*. This weekly newspaper carried national as well as local news.

These were the times during which our black people were seeking a way out of the looming predicament in which we found ourselves. Less than a decade later, my husband became a leader in the political "fusion" movement. As he stated in his newspaper, the experiment of Reconstruction had demonstrated that the blacks could not change the system alone.

"Oh Lizzie, I see the handwriting on the wall for the demise of the Republican Party."

"Have you discussed this with Daddy?" I asked anxiously.

"Yes, and he's not quite there yet. He doesn't want to admit that the safety and success of the Negroes of South Carolina lie in conciliation, and not in antagonism, in their dealings with the whites on state issues. But we've seen what's been happening over the last fourteen years."

During the 1888 election season, Sam helped organize the Fusion Party of Republicans, Democrats and nonaligned white and blacks. The Fusion ticket was successful in our county elections, and Sammy easily won re-election on both Republican and Fusion tickets. But, for the first time in nearly two decades, white Democrats were elected to office in Beaufort County. And that was a harbinger of things to come.

I'm very proud of my husband's active participation in our church. As a staunch Presbyterian, he studied the scripture and became an Elder. There was no black Presbyterian Church in Beaufort after the war. So, even though my Daddy was a founding member of the First African Baptist Church, Sammy and I both felt called to establish another black church in our hometown. The half-dozen church organizers were mostly family members and close friends. We joined together to build a tiny Gothic Revival style predominately black church on 602 Carteret Street, and we named it the Berean Presbyterian Church.

Of all the positions Sammy held, I believe his favorite one was Postmaster of Beaufort, which he occupied from 1896 to 1899. He had just lost his seat as Clerk of Court, so Daddy stepped in to get President William McKinley's attention. Acting on my father's recommendation, President McKinley appointed Sammy to this post.

───

The single event that changed my father's outlook on life was meeting Annie Elizabeth Wigg, when he was forty-two years old. Annie was a beautiful thirty-four-year-old public school teacher from Charleston. She had grown up in an entirely different world than Daddy. Interestingly, Annie studied at the same school as my husband.

Sam was sixteen years of age when Francis Cardozo opened the *Saxton School* for black students in Charleston. Annie Wigg was just ten, but they were students there at the same time. When that school was later moved to its present site, it was re-named the *Avery Normal Institute*.

From the beginning, our family watched Annie and Daddy's love blossom. She brought back the joy Daddy needed. They complimented each other so well. Happiness had returned to our lives, and the whole family rejoiced when they married on April 9, 1890.

Annie Wigg was a breath of fresh air to our household, where Daddy and Sarah had long struggled to bring comfort to each other after Mama's death. Annie was born in Savannah, Georgia, on August 24, 1856, and was the second child of Archibald and Susan Morell Wigg's four children. She studied in private schools in Charleston and at the *Avery Normal Institute* under Francis Cardozo, our family's close friend and mentor. Both of her parents died before Annie's wedding, but we now considered her an important part of our family.

Following the pattern I had set with my 1877 wedding, Daddy scheduled his second marriage ceremony at the First African Baptist Church with the reception in his Prince Street home. It was so magnificent that even the liberal newspaper, the *News and Courier*, gave a very positive review of their wedding.

> *The bride is an exceedingly handsome woman of respectable connection, and the interest felt in her was attested by the large assemblage of whites as well as colored people who attended the church to witness the ceremony, performed at the First African Baptist Church.*
>
> *The bride was elegantly attired in white silk, with a lace overdress entrain and an elegant flowing veil.*
>
> *The residence of the groom, only one block from the church, was brilliantly illuminated, and thither the bridal party with their many friends repaired, and the celebration of the nuptials was concluded by an expensive and elegant supper. The entire community extended to the happy couple their warmest congratulations.*

Naturally, Samuel and others remarked that the newspaper might have used similar words to describe our wedding, but they had ignored our nuptials thirteen years before. We believe it was due to the changed political climate. By 1890, my father was no longer an active political candidate, and the Democrats had long solidified their control over the state, except for Beaufort County. Now the Democratic *News and Courier* could afford to exhibit a measure of benevolence toward Robert Small's wedding.

Reverend Pollard, of the St. Mark's Episcopal Church in Charleston, performed the wedding ceremony. Annie's best friend, Ellen Craft, was her bridesmaid. Ellen later became the godmother to Annie and Daddy's son, William.

Their only child, William Robert Smalls (christened William Robert Wigg Smalls), was born on February 27, 1892, in the master bedroom of our Prince Street house. Samuel and I had our seventh child, Albert Barnes Bampfield, in 1890, so these two boys were very close in age and became fast friends. Our life was fast-moving and full, but we were all happy.

~

Daddy's last major political role was to be one of six black members of the 1895 State Constitutional Convention. He unsuccessfully opposed efforts to disenfranchise African Americans. This convention took away the right of black men to vote and laid the groundwork for the South's *Jim Crow* laws. My father was the only delegate who refused to sign the blatantly racist new constitution.

He did, however, leave the world with this well-delivered last public speech: *My People Need No Defense,* which he gave in response to attacks on his character.

> *"My people need no special defense, for the past history of them in this country proves them to be the equal of any people anywhere. All they need is an equal chance in the battle of life."*
>
> *Robert Smalls, November 1, 1895*

THIRTY-SIX
Elizabeth

Annie, Sarah, Daddy, Sammy and I were all settled in the rockers on the front porch. We were grateful for the little breeze that came up from the Beaufort River. We all appreciate late September and October and the relief that comes after the hot summer weather.

Sammy spoke first. "Do y'all realize just how blessed we are?"

Daddy nodded. "Indeed we do. Health, love, children, grandchildren. Oh my, we do not want for anything, do we?"

I looked at him and giggled. "How about more children? I know Sammy would like that, and I believe little Willie needs more playmates."

Sam laughed as he took a sip of lemonade. "As long as the good Lord gives us the means, we will welcome who ever He sends us, right Sweetie?"

He was correct. We had two older servants who lived in our homes to help care for our everyday needs. All the children were healthy and happy. Daddy's work was running smoothly and gave him extra time to manage some personal properties he owned. In the Prince Street house, he helped install an artesian well and pump. Heat was supplied by six fireplaces and a wood-burning cooking stove, as well as a coal-burning stove. He was happy with the new kerosene lamp lighting, and was especially fond of his beautiful chandeliers.

Annie had given Daddy a new lease on life. They recently established a routine that began at 7 a.m., after the ringing of the town bell. They rose and bathed and then ate their hot breakfast together. Fortunately, they both liked hominy grits, which they consumed almost daily with hot bread, eggs, pancakes, muffins or biscuits. Then Daddy walked to his office at 9 a.m., and Annie decided on her plans for the day.

When Daddy arrived at the Customs House, his office messenger, Henry Garrett, raised the U.S. and the Customs flags. Daddy's deputy, Julius Washington, lived across Prince Street and rented the house from Daddy. Daddy began his series of duties as Customs Collector, including inspections in Beaufort Bay of the vessels coming from foreign ports carrying wood, phosphates and cotton from overseas. After his lunch, which he normally ate at the drugstore near his office, (where he was the only black person served), he conducted personal business and did his paperwork from the morning's ships. The office closed at 4:00 p.m. with a ceremonial lowering of the flags, and my father walked home, to be met by Annie and little Willie.

Then his little family sat down to dinner, often joined by Sammy, me and our children, between 4:30 and 5:00 p.m. We seldom had red meat, because we all preferred seafood, especially shrimp. Our cook often prepared a delicious stew (shrimp mull) that everyone loved. We ate turkeys, chickens and geese that ran free in the back yard. Daddy seldom drank alcohol then, preferring an English lime juice that he got from ships arriving from Great Britain. In the warm months, he preferred iced tea and lemonade.

Then, we retired to the living room or the porch and had our reading and discussion time. Newspaper articles were often read aloud by one of us, (Annie and Sarah enjoyed doing that) and the young children played games or just ran around the yard together. Daddy was so proud of the painting of *The Planter*, hanging on his living room wall. He loved to share stories about that ship and his many adventures as her captain.

When Sarah was home, my father sometimes dictated letters and speeches to her. She still worked for him, even though they were no longer in Washington. Some days Sarah played the piano and we sang Daddy's favorite songs. "Auld Lang Syne" was his favorite, but also loved spirituals, and we knew many from church. Around 9:00 p.m., my family and I returned to our house, while Daddy and Annie locked up, closed the shutters and blinds and retired.

These were very happy times in our lives. During the summer, we went boating, horseback-riding, and even swimming. Daddy liked all three sports and would usually join us. He also raced a trotter, Major Beaufort, at several meets around the state. His coachman drove the sulky, and Daddy proudly watched his horse run and sometimes win.

My father adored his son. Little Willie asked for pets, so Daddy got him some dogs and several kittens, who quickly became tame cats. My children also had their pets, and the youngest ones would sometimes bring their animals over to "play together." In my house, the children helped out by feeding and caring for their animals, but Daddy didn't ask Willie to do this.

Once I asked him a question about his youth. "Daddy, do you remember how Mr. McKee treated you as a young boy?" I wondered.

He looked up from his newspaper. "What do you mean, Lizzie?"

"Well, you and Mama have told me that he doted on you in his own way, always making sure you were happy.

And I see you doing that with your son. It's a wonderful relationship to watch, and I believe that Mr. McKee was so instrumental in your upbringing. After all, you lived almost twelve years under his roof."

Daddy nodded. "I do think about those days and my strong feelings for him. I loved him, Lizzie. He was the father I never had. I guess I want my son to know how important he is and how much Annie and I love him."

"He knows that, Daddy. Even at his age, he sees you as the stately General Smalls. And I am delighted that he understands how much you adore his mother. Willie has everything you could ever wish for him."

We were standing on the porch together one warm afternoon. Looking down toward the water, we watched a pair of pelicans gliding low over the small waves, searching for their dinner.

"You know Lizzie, we can't see what's in store for us. All we can know is what kind of people we want to be."

Smiling, he added, "Thanks to Annie, I know that grace, hope and love will be the foundation of our son's life," he whispered.

"Daddy, I would give the thanks to the Lord, who has given each of us so much." At that very moment, Janet, my two-year-old daughter, tottered over to me, arms outstretched and laughing. Willie and Annie were right behind her.

"Mama, I love you," she sang out. "You too, Grandpa."

My heart was brimming over with love.

THIRTY-SEVEN
Robert

While I was at the 1895 Constitutional Convention in Columbia, Sarah sent word to me that Annie was very ill. *Please come home as soon as you can, Daddy,* she wrote. *We need you.* I left that afternoon, and found my Annie in bed with a terrible headache and abdominal pain. The doctor had just left, but we called him back.

"Captain Smalls, I'm very sorry that I cannot diagnose an illness, even though I've done several tests on her. She has a high fever and we're treating that. She has told me that she's very nervous about the violence happening around the country."

I held her cool hand in mine. "Annie sweetheart, please tell me where it hurts."

She gave me a weak smile. "My head hurts, my stomach is in knots, and I have no appetite." She struggled to sit up in bed. "Oh my love, I just needed to see you. And now that you're here, I'll get better."

I comforted her as best as I could, but became alarmed when she told me the political pressure of our country was weighing heavily on her mind, and, that she couldn't stop thinking about it. "It's like a constant nightmare, and it happens almost every night when I go to sleep," she trembled, squeezing my hand. "I'm frightened that the 1895 Constitution Convention you're attending will be violent and deaths will occur. Oh Robert, please be careful."

"I will stay here with you as long as you need me, dear Annie."

Over the next few days she seemed to slowly crumble, and it looked like nothing we did helped her. She didn't want to eat and told us she could feel her energy gradually flowing away.

"Oh Annie, what can we do for you?" I asked her. Tears streamed down my face as I furiously swiped at them.

"Just hold me, my love. And pray."

The following afternoon, just as the skies were darkening, she asked me to climb into bed and hold her.

"Robert, I love you and Willie so much. Please take very good care of him." She focused directly on my eyes. "Will you promise me that?"

"Don't talk like that, Sugar. You'll get better and we'll both care for him together."

Holding her close, I added, "I'll sing you to sleep and you'll feel much better in the morning."

She smiled and wrapped her thin arms around my chest. A few hours later, she whispered, "Robert, thank you for giving me Willie. I love you." Her voice arose in a little sob. Those were her last words.

After her funeral service at the First African Baptist Church, we buried Annie in the Tabernacle Baptist Cemetery. We placed her right next to Hannah, and I went home and fell apart. I took to my bed and stayed there for several days. I don't remember eating, but I remember sleeping for hours on end.

The day I got up from my bed, Sarah told me that my son Willie, realizing his mother was gone, hid himself in a closet in the clothes hamper. Sammy had to coax him out, and then Willie followed him closely for the rest of the day, clinging to his hand. He even slept at Lizzie's house because he wasn't sure I would be there when he woke up the next day.

I made sure to spend a lot of time with Willie before I returned to the convention in Columbia. I knew I had to go back because there was immediate work to do for my people and my state. Later, people told me that during my troubled and grieving state of mind, I gave my best speech ever. Someone named it: *My People Need No Special Defense*. I have read the printed version in several articles over the years and still find it strong and convincing, although I barely remember speaking those powerful words. Grief wreaks havoc on the mind.

I left Sarah in charge of Willie, knowing she had the temperament and deep love to help him recover from the terrible loss of his mother and the abrupt absence of his father. I don't remember much about the rest of that convention, but I remember the overpowering peace I felt when I arrived back home to my family.

Our little family of three got along quietly and peacefully. Sarah took excellent care of her little brother, and Lizzie helped us a great deal, checking on us every day. Willie slept with me in my large bed and we were comforted by each other's presence. We ate dinner at the usual time, often with Lizzie, Sam and my grandchildren, and then we enjoyed reading/family time until about 8 p.m. I would build a fire in the large fireplace in the bedroom, and then tell my son stories of adventure, war, the escape, etc. that were milestones in my life. He learned so much about his mother and Hannah, as well as Lizzie and me.

Frederick Douglass, always my faithful friend, paid me several visits. One time he brought his grandson, Joseph Douglass, who played the violin. Willie was delighted with this new friend, and of course wanted to play the violin too. He learned slowly over the next two years. He also studied the piano under Sarah's careful guidance. Sarah taught Willie to dance, which he loved. Sometimes we gathered together with Lizzie and her family to play music, dance and sing. What happy, sweet memories I have of those musical moments!

Willie's formal education began in 1896 at age four, when his sister Sarah took him to Orangeburg. She was given a position on the new state college's faculty. She enrolled him in the kindergarten division of the college. When she married in 1900, she made plans to move to Pueblo, Colorado, with her husband, Dr. Jay Williams. Willie was almost nine years old then, and I brought him back home with me. I was delighted to have him in Beaufort again, even though Sarah was in Colorado. However, that marriage was short-lived, and she too, returned home. She was a teacher in a school I founded in Beaufort some years ago. Willie attended that school, just two blocks from our house. In a few years, Sarah became principal of the school. Other family members also studied there, but they were not allowed to call her "Aunt Sarah" in school. She insisted they address her as "Miss Smalls," just like the other children. My son Willie also called her "Miss Smalls" during school hours.

He joined the Allens' Brass Band—the same one I founded years earlier for my political campaign. He was the youngest member and the only child. Willie decided he wanted to play the clarinet, so my friend Allen taught him how. They played on Memorial Day (and other holidays), at parades, funerals, and anytime people asked them. During the funerals, they began with slow tunes on the way to the cemetery. On the way back, they'd liven up their music with "These Dry Bones Shall Rise Again."

When Willie was eleven years old, we decided to send him to Boston. Fortunately, our good friend Mrs. Ariana Sparrow offered to board him in her home. This was the woman Lizzie lived with when she attended school in West Newton, MA. Mrs. Sparrow was very happy to now have Lizzie's younger brother living in her home, and Lizzie was able to visit them twice during his time there.

After grammar school, Willie went to Washington, D.C., where he attended the Academy at Howard University. Then I enrolled him in the Armstrong Technical High School, and after that, he went to the University of Pittsburgh. I was very supportive of his higher education, and I kept up my correspondence with him during that time.

My preference would have been for Willie to study and graduate from West Point or Annapolis. I even wrote a letter to President William Howard Taft, because I knew him and campaigned for him. The letter was written to request an appointment for Willie.

> *Seeing by the papers that there is a large number of vacancies in both the Army and Navy for want of students at West Point and Annapolis, and having no member of Congress to whom I might recommend my son for appointment to either of these Academies as a student, and at the same time knowing that you have a certain number of these appointments to both of these Institutions, and that the practice has been, and I am informed still is, that the President generally appoints the sons of those who have or are serving in the Army*

or Navy, I respectfully recommend for your consideration, my son William R. Smalls.

As it turned out, Willie told me he preferred the University of Pittsburgh, and I didn't argue. He earned his bachelor's degree there and went on to the University of Chicago, where he secured his master's degree in social work. We were all very proud of him!

My sweet daughter, Sarah, began to suffer asthma during the summer months. When she couldn't come to the dining table, I tried to encourage some of my grandchildren next door to join Willie and me for dinner. Around the same time, I realized I was also not as well as I had hoped. My doctor, after conferring with several others, diagnosed me with *Diabetes Mellitus*, also called the "sugar disease."

A specialist from Washington, D.C. came by to visit me and explained the origin.

"Congressman Smalls, your local doctor has told you that you have a high sugar level in your bloodstream. The name "Diabetes Mellitus" comes from a mixture of Greek and Latin, and it means "to pass through." We've just discovered the role of the pancreas and its impact on this disease. We recommend a diet low in carbohydrates and sugar and high in fats and protein."

Our cook was instructed not to feed me certain foods, and the list grew longer as I aged. I obeyed for a while, and slowly realized how much I missed my sweets and breads. So I added them back in smaller portions, but still tried to follow the doctor's orders. Sometimes, my stubborn nature just needed to be harnessed.

THIRTY-EIGHT

Elizabeth

My children were resting with me in the living room on this stormy afternoon. They had done their school work, played a game or two and even read books they enjoyed, but they were tired, restless and irritable. All nine were in the room, even the youngest two, Helen and Ariana.

Raindrops pelted the window panes, drizzling against the glass and blurring my view of the lightning that sizzled across the sky. It illuminated the garden with its garish white light. To the west, thunder rolled ominously over the land.

Suddenly Robbie jumped up. "Mama, why don't you write a book about our family?"

Caught by surprise, I gave him a quick answer. "Who would want to read about us?"

My daughter, Yaddie, now sixteen and an avid reader, expressed her opinion. "Oh yes, Mama! Your life is so interesting and you and Daddy and Grandpa have done so many exciting things. I really think you should. And, we'll help you by collecting important papers and giving you ideas and…"

I laughed lightly. "Well, those family members have done important things, but my story isn't so fascinating," I told her.

"What? Mama, you had eleven children, you escaped slavery with your mother and father and now you're the

Beaufort postmistress—the first female ever to hold the position!"

My daughter, Sarah, entered the conversation to express her agreement, and I noticed how her eyes lit up. At twenty, she was already a beautiful and smart young lady, and she kept a close watch on all of us.

I had never considered writing a book. I didn't know what to tell my children for a long moment, and they respected my silence. Perhaps they were trying to read my thoughts.

Suddenly I thought of Sammy, and wanted him by my side. We were all still grieving him, and had been for over a year. His unexpected death occurred on Christmas Eve of 1899, a little more than a year ago. Sammy was working in his Beaufort office, and I think he probably felt tired and laid his head down on the desk to rest. That's how we found him. The autopsy showed that his heart simply stopped beating. None of our family members knew that he had a heart condition.

Because it was over the Christmas holiday, it was heartbreaking, especially for our children. It was a very difficult time for all of us, yet I knew I needed the strength to keep our home a peaceful place for them. That's what Sammy taught me, and I felt his presence in my heart. He guided me through the worse moments. Thankfully, we had Daddy and Sarah living next door, and Willie was often around to help us heal.

Moreover, Sammy and I lost our eleventh child, Samueletta, in infancy, only a few months before Sammy passed. Our baby, Hannah, had died in infancy some years back. Those loses are forever etched in our hearts. They say children are resilient, but how resilient are we as parents? I probably will never truly understand just how much their siblings' deaths affected us all.

They watched me silently, studying my expression. I smiled slowly as several of them moved over to sit down beside me. Lizzie placed one of her little hands over mine. I found my voice. "Dears, I am thinking of what Robbie suggested. It may be just what we need to keep the lives of Daddy, Gramma Liddy, and my Mama and others we have loved close to our hearts. Why don't we start making notes about what we want to write? And I mean all of us, for possibly, this project of love could help each one of us recover from our losses."

"How, Mama?" asked Lizzie, bewildered.

"Well Lizzie, when we write about someone we love, we can read about that person for years to come, and every time we read their story, we remember them with pleasure."

Flinging her arms around me, Lizzie looked into my face and smiled kindly. "Oh Mama, now I understand," she said softly. "Some things are a gift, even though you don't get to keep them."

Although the rain continued, it seemed that the afternoon conversation had lifted our spirits, and together, we looked forward to starting this new family project.

Daddy's health continued to deteriorate, and his happy spirit seemed to weaken over the next few months. He knew that getting back into politics on some level was the answer to his malaise, so he worked with Booker T. Washington on his new project.

The black community was divided nationwide in deciding how to reverse the rush toward relegation of their race to second-class citizens. On one side, Daddy's highly respected friend, Booker T. Washington, emphasized education: especially trade and vocational training. His *Tuskegee Normal and Industrial School for Negroes* had been doing just that for almost a quarter of a century, and it was widely recognized by both black and white audiences.

Other leaders of black institutions of higher learning followed Washington's example. Thomas Miller advocated the acceptance of social inferiority, arguing that "there is no such thing as social equality anywhere in the world."

Daddy joined this growing group of leaders who aimed at, and expected to achieve, all the enjoyment of domestic happiness that belonged to free and unrestrained citizenship. Basic education for blacks was always high on his political agenda. He continued to protest the injustice to blacks, but no longer went beyond a speech or a letter. And he was often the one who cooperated with whites to get whatever small gains he could. He used his power in Beaufort County, where he might be able to control the diminishing Republican vote.

For over a decade, Daddy and Booker T. Washington corresponded with each other. Booker T. visited him in Beaufort several times over those years. Daddy praised him for his noble efforts for the betterment of the race. Both had established schools in their own areas, and helped each other when needed. Daddy liked to say about his school: "It was the first public act of my life to work for the establishment of these schools in Beaufort."

He walked over to our house late one afternoon, to talk before dinner. "Lizzie, I've finally been invited to Yale University to speak to a Phi Beta Kappa meeting. Do you think I should speak about *The Planter* incident of forty-four years ago?"

I nodded and smiled at him, knowing he would do just that, no matter my opinion. "Of course, Daddy.

And certainly about the sad state of Republican politics in South Carolina."

Dr. Crum came down from Charleston to check on him and treat him for an infected corn. He removed one of Daddy's toes in his home. He also removed a foot bone. Then he sent Daddy to the Freedmen's Hospital in Washington, D.C. for further treatment of his foot, inflammation of his veins, and his diabetes. After this trip, Daddy always walked with a limp. New complications affected his health from that time on. All of this happened in 1906, the year Daddy was the state party vice-chair for the local 1906 election.

Daddy attended the executive committee meeting in Columbia on March 29, 1906. He also went to a later meeting in mid-June, after he was elected as an at-large delegate to the national convention at Chicago. William Taft was easily elected president in 1908, and my father continued to find fault with his policies. He felt they supported segregation, and other practices to suppress the black citizens.

Shortly after the election, resulting in Theodore Roosevelt's win, Booker T. Washington wrote to Daddy to forward comments he had received from Taft's Treasury Secretary McVeagh, "expressing the deepest regret that you have been removed from office." He was referring to his "uncertain" re-appointment as Customs Collector. Daddy's letter of thanks to Booker T. Washington summarized how he wished his last government service to be remembered.

"Lizzie, this is a matter of great importance to me, because my term as Customs Collector will expire in June, 1910, and I am seeking re-appointment. Even the Secretary of the Treasury, Franklin McVeagh, has reported that 'there is an understanding that as long as he lives and is able to perform the duties, he is to remain in office.'"

I nodded. "I think that will happen, Daddy. But you are seventy years old, and should think about enjoying the rest of your years here, in Beaufort, as a retired man."

Daddy laughed out loud. "I enjoy my work, and Beaufort is the place where I want to be."

He wrote to President Taft and said he would visit him at the White House to discuss the customs job. Daddy appeared at the White House on June 14, 1910, but was not admitted. He was back in Washington again in August, for hospital treatment, and looked into his re-appointment. When he heard nothing, he expressed his feelings. *"I haven't lost sight of the fact that I am a Negro, notwithstanding the fact that a hundred and odd of the leading Democrats have signed a special petition headed, 'regardless of politics,' recommending my appointment."*

Daddy continued his duties until a successor was appointed. He was offered and declined President Taft's proposal of the ambassadorship to Liberia in late 1910.

I feel gratified to know that I have lived and so conducted my office, with the assistance of my competent deputy Julius Washington, for all these years, and have not had a single complaint, either of the transactions of the collectorship or of my deputy. During the twenty odd years I have held the position of collector, I have succeeded to so manage affairs so that when I leave it, I will do so with credit to myself, my family and the race...when we go out of office, we go clean. So when the excellent history of the Tuskegee and the Negro shall be written, the Customs House at Beaufort, while conducted by colored men, can be easily attached to the top or bottom, for whatever inspiration it may be to the race.

I found a copy of his letter to Booker T. Washington about a year later. The words were so powerful I needed to remember them forever. Every time I read them, my eyes filled with tears. My Daddy was such a formidable man in his unpretentious way.

THIRTY-NINE

Elizabeth

After Sammy's passing, President Theodore Roosevelt appointed me to his position as the Beaufort postmaster, or in my case, "postmistress." I was very grateful for this honor. I knew what to do and how to do it, since Sammy had taken me to work with him from time to time. Fortunately, like Sammy, I really enjoyed this post and worked there until the political winds of 1908 caused my removal.

I realized it was necessary to have an income to support my family, and I didn't want to ask Daddy to help me, since he was experiencing his own problems. Remembering my happy times and fond recollections of the Penn School, I decided to pay them a visit. I hadn't returned to St. Helena Island since my trip a few years back with my best friend, Renata, and her family.

There were two teachers I knew who still worked at the Penn School, and I found the opportunity to speak with them. They introduced me to the new principal of the school, Miss Rosa B. Cooley, who received me warmly.

"Miss Elizabeth, if you would like to work with us at the Penn School, we can certainly find you a position," smiled Miss Cooley. "In fact, I'm presently looking for another secretary, and I've often heard how good you are at correspondence and organization. You are highly regarded in this school."

"Oh thank you very much, Miss Cooley," I answered self-consciously. "That means so much to me."

She hired me that same day. It was a perfect fit for me, and the work reminded me of my days in Washington, D.C. with Daddy.

At that point I could not know I would only hold this position for the next two years.

∽

Sammy would be so proud of our children. Our oldest, Julia, led the way in the line of upward mobility. Both of us wanted her to attend the Institute for Colored Youth in Philadelphia, where she graduated at the top of her class in the teaching profession. Our second child, Sarah, who was named after her Aunt Sarah, was also educated at the Institute for Colored Youth in Philadelphia. She married Edward Meyer, an accountant in the navy at Bremerton, Washington. They had a boy and a girl, and brought them to Beaufort to meet the family.

Maria (Yaddie) graduated from Barber-Scotia College, and married Charles S. Simpson, a physician, who attended the Shaw University Medical School in North Carolina. They moved to Beaufort, where he practiced medicine. I was able to see them often, and eventually, they purchased the Smalls' house at 501 Prince Street.

Robert (Robbie) Smalls Bampfield was named for his maternal grandfather. He was educated at Johnson C. University, and later joined the U.S. Army and became a lieutenant. Some years later, in World War II, he was wounded in action and received a Purple Heart.

Albert was one of Daddy's favorite grandchildren. He was close in age to Daddy's son Willie, so Albert spent a lot of time at the Smalls' home. Willie told us that once Daddy brought them both elegant suits from a Washington, D.C. trip. He attended public schools in Beaufort and then received a bachelor's degree from Johnson C. Smith University.

Our remaining children were younger and lived with me in Beaufort. This pleased Daddy greatly, because he always wanted his family close, especially during his final years. By 1914, his health had deteriorated further—a combination of the effects of wartime malaria, rheumatism, phlebitis and diabetes. He was confined to his bed, which we moved to the middle of the house, so he could look out on to Prince Street.

"What's the matter with me, Lizzie?" he asked me late one afternoon. His soulful eyes were puzzled, pleading for an answer.

I knew he had asked Sarah the same question. She had been his main caretaker during his final years, and they were very close. I didn't know what she told him.

Sinking into a chair beside him, I forced a smile and told myself to breathe. "Daddy, it is part of growing old." I spoke softly, "and it will reach us all, if we are fortunate."

"Fortunate?" he argued. "I wouldn't wish this on anyone." His dark eyes flashed with annoyance.

I considered his words before I answered. "Think about it Daddy. If you hadn't made it to this age, you would have missed out on a lot of family adventures, and watching your children and grandchildren grow up." I reached for his hands and held them.

"Just look outside, Daddy. The sun is sinking and the clouds above are turning purple and midnight blue. How beautiful is that!"

Daddy nodded. "You are right, my daughter. I'm a blessed man, in spite of my infirmities. And I shall die a proud man."

"Of course you shall, Daddy. Look at all the people who look to you as their leader."

His gaze lingered on my face, and he gave me his sweet smile. "Some have called me 'the leading colored man in South Carolina.' I wonder who will be next."

I couldn't respond right away. I felt tears rushing to my eyes and struggled to fight them. Since I couldn't speak, I nodded instead.

Finally, I turned to him. "Nobody will replace you, Daddy. Your nature has always been to accept what you could not change, with generally good humor, and perhaps to wait for another chance. You are unique. You're not only a Union hero, but an American hero."

I had mourned my mother, my grandmother, two of my daughters, and my husband. I suffered deeply through each of their deaths. With Daddy, it was different. I had loved him too long, and knew the pain of losing him would cut right through my heart and into my soul. With his death, all of my beloved elders would be gone.

But I was wrong. Daddy's spell over me remained strong and warm, even after his body cooled. I sat with him, holding his hand, and letting the sounds of the night envelope me: the cicadas and hoot owls—sounds we often shared together.

I prayed aloud and he heard me, smiling gently and nodding from time to time. Daddy, whose life had been filled with danger, pain, heartache, resignation and loss, was leaving all that behind for a better place. I felt an unexpected surge of happiness for him, knowing that the pain was gone. He left me softly, as I prayed he would.

Robert Smalls closed his eyes at 1:30 a.m. on February 23, 1915, with his children and grandchildren by his side. Daddy was seventy-six years old. Together, our family planned his funeral, and contacted the many African Americans across the Sea Islands who, for decades, had looked to Daddy as their leader. We wanted them to celebrate his life with our family.

A record crowd of black and white mourners paid their respects at his funeral. It turned out to be the largest funeral Beaufort had ever seen. It was held at the First African Baptist Church, where Daddy had been a member for more than ten years. Three ministers asked permission to speak and acknowledge Daddy's life. An elder of the Methodist Episcopal Church spoke of his many achievements, especially on behalf of the African Americans. His good friend Booker T. Washington, now an old man himself, attended. A prominent citizen of Beaufort read telegrams from Daddy's friends across the country who could not attend.

Booker T. stood, aided by family members, to read an epitaph penned by Daddy and given to him on their last visit. It read in part: *During the twenty odd years I have held the position of Customs Collector, I have succeeded to manage affairs that when I leave it, I will do so with credit to myself, my family and the race.*

The music played and the songs sung were Daddy's favorites, including *Shall We Meet Beyond the River?* And of course, the Allen's Brass Band (the one Daddy began years ago) led the procession as friends and family carried Daddy's coffin to the nearby Tabernacle Baptist churchyard, where he was buried between Hannah and Annie.

His death was covered in the *New York Age,* which called him "one of the race's most noted characters."

Daddy had found the way to envision a better life for himself, for his family, and for his country. His was the best of the American spirit. He never lost the faith his mother gifted to him as a small child.

FORTY

Elizabeth

After settling my father's affairs, the younger children and I moved to Charlotte, North Carolina, where we had some Bampfield relatives. My sister, Sarah, came with us, and together, we began a new life. As each of the children married, we doted on and loved on their children.

We found friends and joined in the community life. We kept up with the affairs of our town and the world, as best as we could. Fortunately, all of us are avid readers. I think back on how Daddy couldn't read throughout his childhood, yet he found a way to learn, and then shared his wisdom with so many. He became a prolific writer and a passionate reader. He taught me how to keep my mind sharp, and now I practice that by remembering all of our family members' birthdays. That becomes tricky, as we are now a large family.

I keep in touch with my children and my brother Willie. He and his wife Marty originally planned a grand wedding ceremony at the Prince Street house, but Daddy was very ill. Instead, they married in Texas and honeymooned in Beaufort, where we had a large family reunion. Willie taught school, and then joined the U.S. Army during World War I. After that, he taught at Morehouse College in Atlanta.

Willie served forty-four years in the Urban League movement and was an official of the Urban League in Ohio, as well as a longtime member and officer of the NAACP. How proud Daddy must be of him! He and Marty have two children, a boy named Robert Smalls, III and a girl named Annie Elizabeth (Anne), after her mother and paternal aunt.

I began losing my sight a few years after moving to Charlotte. It was difficult for me to have a handicap, and I'm quite certain it affected my personality at first. Eventually, I became accustomed and now I tell people that if I hadn't lost my sight when I did, I wouldn't be here today. It forced me to slow down at a time when I wouldn't have stopped for anything. God works in strange, yet formidable ways.

My family is the most important treasure I have, and I hold them close. Seven living children, fourteen grandchildren and fifteen great-grandchildren are my gifts from above. I began living with my youngest daughter, Ari Boulware, during the winter months in Durham, North Carolina. In the spring, I return to my own home in Charlotte.

There are many young people throughout the Carolinas who call me "Mama Lizzie." They have been working with me to finish up the "book" we started writing many years ago. Shortly after Sammy died, my son Robbie suggested I write my life story. After some deliberation, I agreed to do it, if my own children would help. They helped, and over the years, we've put our life stories together in a family memoir called *"Blessed."* I have the original, and we've made copies for all of our family members, and a few of our good friends.

So often, because I am now in my late nineties, people will ask me what advice I'd give to young people today.

I've come up with an answer: *The main thing is doing deeds of kindness, helping the needy, and caring for those who are in distress. In other words, as the Good Book tells us, be the hands and feet of God.*

AFTERWORD

Elizabeth Smalls Bampfield was the daughter of a daring sea hero, Robert Smalls, and Hannah Jones Smalls. She passed away on March 19, 1959, in Charlotte, North Carolina, at the age of 101. She is buried in Mercy Cemetery, Beaufort, South Carolina, next to many of her family members.

Elizabeth was given a commemorative birthday celebration, attended by family and close friends, when she turned 95. She had been blind for twenty years and her hearing was impaired by age 85. She was loved and highly respected by many, both in Durham and in Charlotte, North Carolina. She lived the final sixteen years of her life in Durham, with her youngest daughter Ari Boulware.

Although she was both sight and hearing impaired, Elizabeth kept up with local and world affairs. She had a strong affection for children and young people, and said that "to keep my mind working," she decided to memorize the birthdays of her fourteen grandchildren, fifteen great-grandchildren and four great-great grandchildren.

Elizabeth Smalls Bampfield is an inspiration and an important part of U.S. Black heritage. She had a clever sense of humor, and a unique knowledge of politics and world events. She left the world a compelling and deep-rooted legacy. Her true story is a loving inspiration to women everywhere.

OBITUARY

Mrs. Elizabeth Smalls Bampfield, age 101, of 306 Mill Rd., passed away at 1:15 pm, Thursday, March 19th, 1959, at 401 Carmel St. She was born February 12, 1858 in Charleston, S.C. daughter of the late Robert and Hannah Smalls. Her early childhood was spent in Beaufort, S.C. where she completed her elementary training. Then she went to West Newton, Mass. to complete her higher training. After which she became secretary to her father Robert Smalls, Congressman from South Carolina. She later married Samuel J Bampfield who served as Clerk of Court and Recorder of Deeds for twenty years in Beaufort, County S. C.

At the death of her husband, she was appointed postmistress by President Theodore Roosevelt. She served two terms in that capacity. Later she served as secretary to Mrs. Rossa B. Cooley, principal of Penn Normal and Industrial School at St. Helena Island, S. C.

She was a member of Biddleville Presbyterian Church. She leaves to mourn their loss five daughters, Mrs. Julia B. Stinson of Charlotte, NC., Mrs. Elizabeth B. Hall of Washington, D.C., Mrs. Janet Davidson of Washington, D.C., Mrs. Helen B. Givens of Charlotte, NC., Mrs. Arianna R Boulware of Durham, NC.; two sons, Robert S. Bampfield of Washington, D.C., and Albert B. Bampfield of Augusta, GA; fourteen grandchildren, fifteen great-grandchildren and four great-great grandchildren.

ACKNOWLEDGMENTS

An author never works in a vacuum. Every writer needs assistance, and finds people who encourage, offer new ideas, and lend a helping hand. My book team deserves endless thanks for their patience, kindness, knowledge, and their willingness to work on my new story.

Tremendous thanks go to Robert Whalen, my friend and editor for this book. We spent many hours together, and he was always available when I needed him. Not only did he edit, but he assisted me on some of the overwhelming research. Bob knows so much about the Civil War, and offered necessary corrections to my story when I went astray. What a delight it was to work with you, Bob!

To Patty Osborne, my loyal, and very intelligent Canadian friend, (of many years) who has been my "bookmaker" for all sixteen of my books. I send you my endless gratitude. You take the book covers, the pictures and the manuscripts and transform them into beautiful books. You encouraged me to publish my very first children's book in 1999, and we're still working together. You are the BEST, Patty. I also want to thank Michal Kozlowski, Patty's associate, who has worked with us on this book and has done an excellent job.

Gini Steele, my dear friend and cover artist, has worked with me creating the covers of seven other books and this new one, and has always performed her magic on them. She was the one who told me about Lizzie Smalls, and talked about her again and again, until I finally agreed to write her story. Gini also accompanied me on the research of the Smalls family in Beaufort. Gini, I remain under your spell and am in awe of your talent. Thank you so much. You also made this challenging cover come to beautiful life.

Extensive research was conducted to find intricate details of Lizzie's story. Grace Cordial, Senior Librarian and Archivist at the Beaufort County Library, was so helpful in finding many useful references for me. Kudos also go to Virginia L. Ellison—Director of Archives and Research at the South Carolina Historical Society Archives. Working with both of you was a pleasure.

I have three wonderful proof readers. Each of them offered me wisdom and support, and made the book read better than I originally wrote it. Interestingly, all three have been or are presently school teachers. Cassandra Gual Reyes has worked with me previously, and I love the fact that my daughter reads and corrects my books before they are even printed. She is currently a second grade teacher in Idaho. Cassandra has always been drawn to the plight of the underprivileged, so I knew this story would resonate with her sense of justice.

One of my besties, Suzi Hassel, has proofed my last five books. She also joined me on two research trips for previous books. She's a pro at finding errors and helping me discover better replacement words. Suzi taught me that reading the manuscript outloud is very helpful. Leigh Kosidowski, my friend and newest proof reader, loves to dive into Civil War history. I've been a "visiting author" at her school, and I applaud her enthusiasm for the written word. Thank you to all three women for being such important members of my team.

I chose the title for this book before I even wrote the first sentence. Lizzie was only four when she became part of "the great escape," because her father knew he had to risk everything for his family's freedom. What a strong woman she became! Her descendants, Michael B. Moore, Gwen Bampfield and Ethel Bampfield Denmark, shared with me glimpses into their great-grandmother's life. Michael selected and sent me family photos to include in the book, which was the best gift I could have received. I was so fortunate to work with them, and their support facilitated the writing of Elizabeth Smalls Bampfield's story. I'm grateful and thankful to each one of you, for sharing your time and personal knowledge to help me write Lizzie's amazing story.

My profound thanks go to my devoted husband Michael. How blessed I am to have a loving, wise, caring and generous man who is happy to do life with me. His constant encouragement is amazing; his love sustains me daily. Thank you, Mike, for believing in me and sharing this journey.

Finally, I give profound thanks to my Lord and Savior. You walk with me every step of the way. Jesus, thank you for the comfort of Your spirit and Your grace. I dedicate this story to You and place it in Your loving arms.

BOOK GROUP DISCUSSION QUESTIONS

1. Describe the kinds of emotions this story evokes in you.
2. Did you enjoy having four narrators telling the story? Could you identify with any of them? If so, how?
3. There are themes of faith and following God's word throughout the story. How important was this to the main characters' lives?
4. The Civil War had a profound impact on the roles and freedom of women. What were some of the changes and how did this surprise you? Can you think of ways these changes continue to impact the lives of women today?
5. Do you feel that Lizzie's memories were accurate and reliable? How does the past affect our future?
6. Evaluate the four central characters' themes of freedom and hope in this story. How would you express their driving force to "be free or die?"
7. Do you enjoy novels about real people and real events? How are they different from historical fiction? Which genre do you prefer reading?
8. People determine what kind of life is worth living. Have you wondered how your choices and decisions have affected your life? Which choices and/or decisions have had the greatest impact on your life?
9. Did you understand the complexity of Reconstruction? How did you feel reading about this time period?
10. After reading Lizzie's story, what are some lessons that you can apply to your own life?

RESOURCES

Primary Sources
Billingsley, Andrew, *Yearning to Breathe Free*, Columbia, South Carolina, University of South Carolina Press, 2007.

Lineberry, Cate, *Be Free or Die*, New York, New York, St. Martin Press, 2017.

Miller Jr., Edward A., *Gullah Statesman, Robert Smalls—From Slavery to Congress*, 1839-1915, Columbia, South Carolina, University of South Carolina Press, 1995.

Newkirk, Pamela, *Letters From Black America*, Garden City, New Jersey, Farrar, Straus & Giroux, 2009.

Sterling, Dorothy, *Captain of the Planter*, New York, New York, Doubleday Publishing, 1958.

Secondary Sources
Bass, Jack, *The Palmetto State: The Making of Modern South Carolina*, Columbia, South Carolina, University of south Carolina Press, 2009.

Bruff, Rebecca Dwight, *Trouble the Water*, Virginia Beach, VA, Virginia Beach Press, 2019.

Coker, P.C., *Charleston's Maritime Heritage 1670-1865*, Charleston, South Carolina, Coker-Craft Publishing, 1987.

Dobbs, Edith M., *Face of an Island*, Charleston, South Carolina, Wyrick & Company Press, Charleston, South Carolina, 1970.

Hagood, Johnson, *Memoirs of the War of Secession*, Columbia, South Carolina, Columbia State Press, 1910.

Rabinowitz, Howard N, *Southern Black Leaders of the Reconstruction Era*, Chicago, IL, University of Illinois Press, 1982.

Trash, Graham, *Beautiful Beaufort by the Sea*, Beaufort, South Carolina, Beaufort Press, 1994.

Uya, Okon Edet, *From Slavery to Public Service: Robert Smalls, 1839-1915*, New York, New York, Oxford University Press, New York, 1971.

Uya, Okon Edet, *Robert Smalls and his Descendants*, New York, New York, The Negro History Bulletin-November, 1947

Westwood, Howard, *Black Troops, White Commanders and Freedmen during the Civil War,* Columbia, South Carolina, SIV Press, 1991.

Vandervelde, Isabel, *Aiken County: The Only South Carolina County Founded During Reconstruction,* Spartanburg, S.C. Reprinted by original publishers. 1998.

Internet and Magazine Articles

www.pbs.org, Gates, Henry Louis Jr., *Which Slave Sailed himself to Freedom? January* 13, 2013

www.historynet.com/magazine/american-civilwar-*The Unbeatable Mr. Smalls, March* 2007

www.hagley.org/library/exhibits/civilwar/smalls/index/ *Robert Smalls: Former Slave and Civil War Hero.* Hagley Museum and Library.

www.wikipedia.org/-Elizabeth Smalls.

www.wikipedia.org/-Robert Smalls.

www.livescience.com, Wolchover, Natalie, *Why did the Democrat and Republican Parties Switch Platforms?*

www.nps.gov/read/learn Presidential Proclamation-Reconstruction. Era National Monument-U/S National Park Service.

www.npgallery.nps.gov/NRHP/GetAsset/NHLS/74001824, Sheire, James, National Register of Historic Places Inventory-Nomination, Penn Center Historic District/Penn School

www.worldcat.org/oclc/33441, Allen, Walter 1840-1907, Governor Chamberlain's Administration in South Carolina; a chapter of reconstruction in the Southern states. New York, Negro Universities Press, 1888.

www.worldcat.org/oclc/17298575, Haworth, Paul Leland, 1876-1963, *The Hayes-Tilden Disputed Presidential Election of* 1876. Whitefish, Montana, 1906.

www.henryshultz.wordpress.com 2015/02/23, Official Report of the Battle of Hamburg, Attorney General of South Carolina, 1876. Accessed March 2015.

www.nytimes.co,/books/00/05/21, Kantrowitz, Stephen, *"Book Review of Ben Tillman and the Reconstruction of White Supremacy,"* New York, New York, *The New York Times,* May 2000 www.jstor.org/stale/27567894, Hennessy, Melinda Meeks, *Racial Violence During Reconstruction: The 1876 Rios in Charleston and Cainhoy, South Carolina Historical Magazine*, Vol 86, No 2 (April 1985)

Holt, Thomas (1979) "Chapter 8": *Black Over White: Negro Political Leadership in South Carolina during Reconstruction*, University of Illinois Press, p. 173-207

Simkins, Francis Butler, *Pitchfork Ben Tillman: South Carolinian*, p. 270.

United States Congress, Robert Smalls-50000502-htpp:/bio/guide/congress/gov/scripts/biodisplay/Biological Directory of the United States Congress.

ABOUT THE ARTIST

This is Gini Steele's eighth historical novel cover art for author Pamela Bauer Mueller. Combining her love of photograph and history, Gini enjoys the challenge of interpreting the old negatives and photographs, then using digital technology to complete the image and create a unique piece of art. Over the years, Gini  and her husband Richard created an extensive collection of photographic images of times gone by. Throughout their work with historical societies, archivists and researchers, they realized there was a need to restore and reproduce these images and make them available, before they became lost forever.

Gini enjoys the challenge of interpreting the old negatives and photographs, using digital technology to complete the image, creating a unique piece of art.

She prints the silver gelatin photographs by hand, one at a time. Once tinting is accomplished, Gini uses digital technology to complete the image, creating a unique art piece.

Gini recently moved to James Island, S.C. with her cat, Penelope Butterbeans. She loved her many years residing in Beaufort, S.C., but now lives closer to her family on James Island. Gini can work anywhere there is beauty and nature.

www.ingramcontent.com/pod-product-compliance
Lightning Source LLC
Chambersburg PA
CBHW071859290426
44110CB00013B/1214